The Flying Tigers

During World War II a group of American fighter pilots roamed the skies over China and Burma, menacing the Japanese war effort without letup. Flamboyant, daring and courageous, they were called the Flying Tigers.

The Tigers, who had been recruited from the Army, Navy and Marines, first saw action as a volunteer group fighting on the side of Chiang Kai-shek's China against Japan. Schooled in the unconventional air-combat tactics of their unorthodox leader, Claire Lee Chennault, they racked up some of the most impressive air-victory records of World War II.

In this book John Toland tells the incredible story of Chennault and his magnificent Tigers, a group of men who performed the impossible.

THE
FLYING
TIGERS

BY JOHN TOLAND
Illustrated with photographs

RANDOM HOUSE: NEW YORK

To Rogers Terrill

Acknowledgments

Numerous agencies, organizations and individuals made this book possible. I would like to thank Dr. Albert Simpson, Margo Kennedy and Clark F. Palmer of the Air University Archives at Maxwell Air Force Base, Alabama; Judge Israel Wice and Charles Romanus of the Office of the Chief of Military History, Department of the Army; Lieutenant Colonel C. V. Glines, Major Gene Guerny and Mrs. Alice Martin of the Magazine and Book Branch of the U.S. Air Force; Lieutenant Colonel Robert Prentiss of the Office, Chief of Information, U.S. Army; Edith Midgette, Office of News Services, Depart-

Acknowledgments

ment of Defense; and Colonel E. R. Mason, Major Fred Mitchell and W. N. Sholl of the Fourth U.S. Army Information Office, Fort Sam Houston, Texas.

Among the libraries which contributed greatly to the book, I should like to mention the Historical Archives in Alexandria, Virginia; the Library of the Office of the Chief of Military History, Department of the Army, Washington, D.C.; and the Air University Library at Maxwell Air Force Base, Alabama.

I am also indebted to many participants in the events related in the book, who told their personal stories. Those who were particularly generous with their time include Joseph W. Alsop, Thomas G. Corcoran, Colonel Ed Rector and David "Tex" Hill. Finally I would like to thank Mrs. Claire Lee Chennault and Colonel Fred C. Milner for reading the manuscript, and the officers and members of the 14th Air Force Association for their assistance.

Contents

The Flying Tigers

Old
Leatherface

1.

The big Pan American clipper took off from Hawaii and headed east for the United States. It was the middle of October, 1940. Almost everyone aboard was well aware that war between America and Japan was brewing, but none more so than a man of fifty who was studying a notebook as if his life depended on it. He was of average size, stocky, muscular and supple. He had dark, stubby hair graying at the temples. His weather-beaten face was rugged and so deeply lined it might have been chipped from rock.

The man's name was Claire Lee Chennault, and he was a former United States Air Corps acrobatic flier and flying school director. After ten years' service he had resigned his captaincy in 1937 to become a colonel, and the foremost ace, in the Chinese air force. For the past three years he had been chief air strategist for Chiang Kai-shek, leader of the Chinese people in the war against Japan.

The fighting had started on a peaceful July night in 1937 when a company of Japanese soldiers suddenly crossed the Marco Polo Bridge outside Peiping and invaded Chinese territory. Chinese soldiers protested and there was an exchange of fire. Japan's long-laid plans to dominate Asia and the islands of the Pacific had officially begun.

China—already disunited by years of civil war—seemed to be completely open to conquest. But Chiang Kai-shek, a former disciple of the great Chinese revolutionary, Dr. Sun Yat-sen, mobilized an army and began a gallant, if apparently hopeless, defense.

Chennault believed that China's war with Japan was also America's. He was sure Japan would eventually turn to the east and attack the United States. So he had volunteered his services to Chiang, and by 1940 the former American captain was affectionately known all over China as "Old Leatherface."

Only a few days earlier, Chiang Kai-shek had summoned Chennault to Chungking. The Chinese air force, said the Generalissimo, was now so feeble it could do little to stem the terrifying bombings. Unless the slaughter was stopped, Chiang Kai-shek was afraid his people would have to surrender.

Claire Chennault (left) chats with Generalissimo and Madame Chiang Kai-shek in front of a building camouflaged with paint.

But he had a last, desperate plan. Why not buy the latest American fighter planes and hire American pilots to fly them? Chennault shook his head. England was now fighting for her life against Nazi Germany and any planes not needed for the United States Army or Navy were being sent to Europe.

Even so the Generalissimo ordered him to fly to America immediately. "Work out the plans for whatever you think you need. Do what you can to get American planes and pilots."

By the time the clipper neared California, Chennault

5

had his plan. And he knew it would work. For three years he had been personally fighting Japanese pilots in his Curtiss Hawk 75. Although only the Chinese leaders knew it, he had already destroyed more planes in combat than any other American. Chennault was confident that young, experienced pilots trained in his unorthodox tactics could knock down five enemies for every loss. A small group of such men, moved around China like a mobile aerial fire department, could stop the Japanese bombings.

A day later Chennault landed in Washington, D.C., where he reported to Dr. T. V. Soong, the Generalissimo's brother-in-law, and the man responsible for getting aid from the United States. Soong said he was having a hard job convincing Americans that the Japanese were daily becoming a greater menace to the United States. Hundreds of young Americans were volunteering to fly for Canada and England, but it had not yet occurred to a single one to volunteer for duty in China.

That same night Soong took Chennault to dinner with two famous journalists—Edgar Ansel Mowrer of the Chicago *Daily News* and Joseph W. Alsop, Jr., of the New York *Herald Tribune*. Chennault shocked them when he reported that the Japanese were using an amazing new fighter plane in China. It was called the Zero and could climb more than twice as fast as the American P-40. It was so maneuverable that it was suicide to engage it in a dogfight. But trained American aviators flying the most advanced American aircraft could be taught how to knock down the Zero.

Chennault outlined his plan but the journalists were as gloomy as Soong. The British legitimately had first priority on the best planes. Chennault's volunteer project, they felt, was doomed to failure.

Chennault refused to be discouraged. He began to visit his old friends still in the Air Corps. They too shook their heads. He told them about the new Zero and handed over detailed information to the War Department listing its capabilities. It had a level top speed of 322 miles per hour and a range of 1,100 miles. It could climb 16,000 feet in six minutes, and carried a cannon and four machine guns. Chennault was politely thanked, but War Department experts claimed it was impossible to build such a plane. And his information was filed and forgotten.

Few in the Air Corps would listen to Chennault's pleas for help. Many high-ranking officers didn't like him and referred to him as "The Prima Donna." He had always disagreed with their theory that high-flying bombers would win the next war. They firmly believed that bombers could not be stopped by enemy fighter planes and didn't even need a fighter escort.

Chennault, like General Billy Mitchell, was never one to speak out quietly or politely. Mitchell, a fiery advocate of air power, had sacrificed his career in a public battle with superior officers who could not see the importance of a mighty United States air force. Chennault was just as fiery and indignant. He had criticized the bomber theory bluntly and loudly, claiming that his superior officers were completely wrong. As could be expected, they now refused to help him.

In the next few weeks, while China was hopefully waiting for help, Chennault toured from coast to coast begging for planes and pilots. To anyone who would listen he talked of the growing danger in the Orient. He predicted that Japan was preparing to seize Singapore, the Dutch East Indies and even America's possession, the Philippines. Few listened. All eyes were focused on Europe and the gallant battle England was waging against Hitler.

Two men did listen. They were Frank Knox, Secretary of the Navy, and Henry Morgenthau, Secretary of the Treasury. At President Roosevelt's cabinet meetings, these two began to plead the cause of Chennault and China.

About this time Chennault was also introduced to a lawyer, Thomas J. Corcoran—better known as "Tommy the Cork." He was one of the brilliant young men who were advising President Franklin D. Roosevelt. Like Dr. Soong and the President he was a graduate of Harvard. For the past year he had been working under cover for the Chinese resistance movement in an organization called "China Defense Supplies."

At their first meeting in Corcoran's apartment Chennault explained, in his slow southern drawl, the situation in China. He unrolled a map and pointed out a number of Chinese airfields far behind the enemy lines.

"You talk about operating airfields way inside Japanese territory," said Corcoran dubiously. "But how's it going to be done?"

Chennault said he had built the fields himself. He knew every curve of the mountains; he knew all the people. "I can jump in and out of these fields at will. I'm surrounded by friends. I can smash the Japs and before they can get at me, I'll be gone."

Corcoran was utterly fascinated by such an unorthodox concept. An ordinary military man would have thought it impossible. This obviously was no ordinary man. And he wasn't just a dreamer. He knew his facts.

After Chennault told about the new Zero, Corcoran said, "But Colonel, we haven't anything to give you. Our P-40 wouldn't stand a chance."

"Not unless I can train my pilots to act *abnormally* in handling the P-40," was Chennault's mysterious reply. "I've studied the capabilities of the Zero. Like every plane it's sacrificed some capacities to attain others." He said he could train pilots to take advantage of the Zeros' weaknesses and shoot them down. But these men would have to be restrained from fighting on terms advantageous to the Zero.

"Get me the right men with the right training and I can teach them to beat the 'superior' Zero with the 'inferior' P-40. My Chinese intelligence network will inform me when the Zeros are on the way, and I'll be up there when they come over the target. I'll wait up above till the Japs are low on fuel. Then I'll attack! My heavier P-40 can dive faster and I'll dive! I won't make the mistake of trying to turn. If I miss I'll go back up for another dive." He leaned forward eagerly. "Throw the

9

Japs off balance like that and you've got 'em."

Corcoran was convinced by the other man's complete confidence, and the next time he visited President Roosevelt he added his plea for Chennault. Roosevelt said he was intrigued with the entire idea but protested that it was illegal. America was not at war with Japan.

In the next few weeks Corcoran and other Chennault supporters kept arguing the cause of China with Roosevelt. At last, in January of 1941—just after listening to one of Corcoran's impassioned pleas—the President decided that the formation of a group of American volunteer fliers, using American planes, was an experiment worth seriously considering. He gave the scheme his tentative approval.

Not long after this Chennault visited the Curtiss-Wright factory in Buffalo, New York, and learned that 100 P-40B Tomahawks were just rolling off the assembly lines. They were scheduled to go to England, but the British were persuaded to relinquish them to Chennault. They would get a later model, much more suitable for combat.

At last, half of Chennault's problems were solved. But getting pilots proved to be an even harder job. General H. H. ("Hap") Arnold, the Chief of the Air Corps, was violently opposed to the whole idea. He told Chennault he would not send a single pilot to any other country without putting up a fight. Chennault got almost the same reception from Rear Admiral Jack Towers, Chief of the Navy's Bureau of Aeronautics. Since there was no other place to get experienced fighter pilots, it looked as

◄ Top: An Allied pilot flies a captured Zero over Australia. Bottom: A Japanese Zero captured by the Flying Tigers stands next to a P-40.

if there would never be an American Volunteer Group in China.

2.

The ordinary man would have given up, but Chennault had fought discouragement all his life. When he was a freshman cadet at Louisiana State University, the Regular Army officer in charge gave him a stern lecture in front of the company and said, "Chennault, you will never make a soldier."

After graduating from college, young Chennault went to normal school and then began to teach at a one-room country school in Athens, Louisiana. The pupils were so unruly that the average teacher lasted less than a term. But Chennault, who was not as old as some of the overgrown farm boys, invited the biggest ones to go out behind the school house with him. Here he fought them with bare knuckles, one by one, and beat them all. Instead of resenting Chennault, the boys became his ardent champions, and discipline was finally achieved at the Athens school.

In the next few years Chennault and his growing family drifted around the South, as he moved from one job to the next. When America declared war on Germany in 1917, he applied for flight training in the Army. Ever since he had seen his first rickety plane, he had wanted to be an aviator. But when he applied he was rejected with the comment, "Applicant does not possess necessary qualifications for a successful aviator."

Undismayed, he applied for the infantry and was soon a first lieutenant. It was not until a few days after the Armistice in 1918 that he finally had his first plane ride —in a Curtiss Jenny. Once in the air, he knew it was his element. Though he was twenty-nine and already the father of four children, he persisted until he was allowed to take flight training.

His fiery temper almost ended his new career before it was under way. His instructor had a habit of momentarily jerking the controls away when Chennault made a mistake. The student became so angry that he finally told the instructor he would refuse to fly the ship the next time it happened. A little later, the instructor jerked the stick away. Instead of taking back the controls as he was supposed to, the stubborn Chennault folded his arms. The Jenny plunged toward the earth. A few feet above a cornfield, the instructor grabbed the stick.

In spite of the instructor's recommendation to "wash out" Chennault, he was given another chance and in a few years became one of the Army's best pursuit pilots. He was strong, wiry and shrewd and had split-second reflexes.

In 1923 Chennault's squadron put on an air show for the citizens of El Paso, Texas. A pilot announced that an aged woman named Grandma Morris had asked to be a passenger in one of their planes. Grannie Morris, covered with long coat and aviator's helmet, was carefully hoisted into the rear cockpit. Then the pilot spun the propeller. The motor started and the plane darted forward, almost knocking the pilot over. The crowd watched in horror as the plane, with only Grannie aboard, clumsily took to the air. They were even more amazed when it suddenly twisted, dived and performed amazing Immelmanns, loop-the-loops and figure eights. When it landed, Grannie Morris jumped agilely to the ground and threw off the long coat. "She" was Lieutenant Chennault.

In the next few years Chennault began to develop his ideas for fighting a war in the air. He angered high-ranking officers, who claimed that pursuit planes could not possibly stop a bombing raid. Though he "shot down" bomber after bomber in maneuvers, his superiors claimed he used unfair tactics.

Chennault even wrote a manual, *The Role of Defen-*

Captain Claire Lee Chennault

sive Pursuit, demonstrating that the methods of World War I dogfighting were obsolete. Fighter planes should operate in pairs, he said—and was promptly ridiculed. All his unorthodox ideas were ridiculed.

To prove that fighters could maneuver in close formation, he formed an air acrobatic team called "Three Men on a Flying Trapeze." For the next three years Chennault and two other pilots performed in perfect formation every known acrobatic trick and some they made up. They looped, spun, double-rolled. They performed wing overs, snap and slow rolls. They even did three-turn tail spins, coming out in precise formation. As a final test, Chennault would tie the three planes together with rope. Again they would go through their acrobatics and land—still tied together.

With every passing year, the outspoken Chennault got into more and more trouble with those who outranked him. He refused to be quiet and persistently argued that more pursuit pilots should be trained—and trained in his tactics.

To make matters worse his health became so bad he was allowed to fly only a two-seater training plane, with another pilot in the front cockpit. When he was finally sent to the hospital, it seemed as if his hectic career as an aviator was over.

At this low point he was offered a job by Chiang Kai-shek to survey the Chinese air force. He would be paid $1,000 a month, plus expenses, and could fly any plane in the Chinese air force. Would he accept?

He settled his large family in Waterproof, Louisiana,

and on April 30, 1937, officially retired from the United
States Army. The next morning he started for China,
apparently heading for oblivion. Yet in a few years, at
the age of fifty-one, he would be recognized throughout
the world as one of the Allies' greatest air heroes.

3.

In February and March of 1941, Roosevelt was pulled
first one way, then another, with regard to a volunteer
air group to fight under Chennault in China. The military leaders argued persuasively that it would be folly
to give up any of the few trained pilots they had. Other
critics of the scheme pointed out that the volunteers
would actually be soldiers of fortune—on the payroll of
Chiang Kai-shek. How would the public react to Americans fighting on a mercenary basis?

Corcoran and the other supporters of Chennault
agreed that public reaction was a great risk. But in
such perilous times it had to be taken. And they were
even more persuasive than the military leaders when
they argued that every pilot sent to China would be the
wisest possible investment in the inevitable war against
the Axis.

On April 15, 1941, the President signed an unpubli-
cized executive order. It authorized reserve officers and
enlisted men to resign from the Army Air Corps, the
Naval and Marine Air services so they could join Chennault's American Volunteer Group.

Since the United States was not at war with Japan

and could not deal openly with China, some unofficial agency would have to arrange everything with absolute secrecy. William Pawley, an international airplane salesman, now made a suggestion. Why not designate his company, which had an assembly plant in China, as the go-between? Everyone agreed that this was a good idea, and the Central Aircraft Manufacturing Company of China (CAMCO) was authorized to hire one hundred American pilots and several hundred ground crewmen to "operate, service and manufacture aircraft in China."

A few days later, commandants of Army and Navy air bases were told that civilians would soon visit their fields to talk with pilots and ground crews. The visitors would have no official standing, yet they were to be given every assistance. And there would be the utmost secrecy. More than one commandant scratched his head in wonder at these strange instructions.

Rutledge Irvine, a retired Navy commander, was chosen by Chennault to recruit at the important Navy air bases. As soon as he arrived at the Naval Air Base in Norfolk, Virginia, he sought out Captain Gus Widhelm, a flight instructor. While the two were discussing the men best qualified for service in China, two young ensigns strolled toward them.

"Here's a couple of guys that'll go with you," said Widhelm.

One was six feet three inches tall, and slender, with blond hair and blue eyes. He walked with a swaying roll as if he had just gotten off a horse. His name was David Lee Hill, but everyone called him Tex. The other was five inches shorter but weighed only a few pounds less. He was solid, muscular. This was Ed Rector, who had played center on his college football team in North Carolina. Both young men were pilots in Bombing 4 Squadron and had just come off the carrier USS *Ranger*.

Irvine brought the two puzzled dive-bombers into an office, pulled down a map and pointed out the last lifeline to China, the Burma Road. "We need volunteers," he said, "to help patrol the Burma Road."

Tex Hill looked at Widhelm, then at Irvine, and said in his slow drawl, "What's this all about?"

"Chennault wants men to fight for China," said Irvine bluntly.

Both young pilots edged forward expectantly. Hill had been trying to get to China for a long time. He had been born in Korea, where his father was a missionary. For him the Orient always had been a magnet.

Edward F. Rector (left) and David Lee Hill

To Rector the opportunity sounded too good to be true. Ever since reading Kipling, he had been intrigued by the Far East. He had heard about Chennault, too, and had respect for his theories of pursuit planes.

Irvine said there might not be much fighting—or there might be a lot. "Chennault wants military pilots," he continued. "He's had bad experience with barnstormers, and he's looking for young guys with a couple of years' flying experience." He explained that they would have to resign their commissions in the Navy. They would be agents for the Chinese government but would take orders only from Chennault. "Some of us feel the United States is getting into a war. Here's an opportunity for fighting experience. And besides, there's good dough in it."

Irvine explained that pilots would get $600 a month. Flight leaders would be paid $675; and squadron leaders would receive $750. "There'll be a bonus—which won't appear in the contract—of $500 from the Chinese government for each Jap plane shot down." The whole project, he said, had been authorized by President Roosevelt. The volunteers would not lose their citizenship, and when the one-year contract expired they could be reinducted into the Navy without losing rank.

Both ensigns were interested in the proposition—more for the adventure than the money. Hill asked, "What if America gets into war?"

"You can resign immediately."

Rector still thought it was too good to be true. It

must be a joke. He looked at Tex Hill. Then both said they would like to go. No papers were signed, however, and soon they sailed again on the *Ranger*. In mid-ocean their squadron flew aboard the SS *Yorktown* and finished the cruise aboard that great carrier.

When Hill and Rector finally returned to Norfolk, they were greeted by Irvine.

"Here're your applications," he said. "Just buck them through your skippers."

But when the commander of their squadron saw the applications he was stunned. "You guys can't leave," he said. "This is a joke!"

Hill and Rector assured him it was not. The enraged squadron commander complained to the air group commander who in turn complained to the skipper of the *Yorktown*. This officer hurried to the Navy Department in Washington, but his protests were quickly stopped by a direct call to the White House.

Late that afternoon Hill and Rector were called to the office of their group skipper. "Boys," he said, "I don't know what's up." He tapped their applications. "This really has high priority." Then he relaxed, wished them good luck and said the ship was throwing a party that night for all the volunteers.

"I'm Really
in Something Hot
Now...."

1.

Tex Hill and Ed Rector took a week's vacation at home, then went to San Francisco and joined twenty-six other volunteer pilots. One of these was a good friend from their own squadron, Allen Bert Christman. After helping Milt Caniff draw "Terry and the Pirates" for two years, Christman had decided to start his own comic strip. He enrolled in the Navy Flying School to get background material. His hero was a daredevil Navy flier, and Christman had already drawn enough strips for about five months. Every time he finished one he would try it out on Hill and Rector.

After approximately ten days of preparations, the

21

volunteers boarded the Dutch ship *Bloemfontaine* and headed west. They all wore civilian clothes and were listed in their passports as acrobats, baseball players, missionaries, vaudeville actors and even embalmers. Tex was a "rancher;" Ed an "engineer."

About a month previously, on July 11, 1941, the first contingent of volunteers—some 150 pilots and ground crewmen—had left on another Dutch ship. Hill and Rector's group was the second, and others would follow. When they were only a day out of San Francisco, word came that the Japanese had invaded Indochina. On awaking the next morning the volunteers were surprised and relieved to find a United States battle cruiser escorting them.

Upon arriving at Honolulu, the skipper of the *Bloemfontaine* was given orders to take a new course. The ship proceeded in a zigzag course to Australia, then to Manila and back to Batavia, Java. While waiting to transfer to another Dutch vessel, Hill and Rector took trips into the lushly vegetated hills. For the first time they felt they were seeing the real Orient: little men pulling huge loads, women carrying great bundles on their heads. Flowers of all colors and shapes bloomed in profusion, and the heat seemed like a blanket.

They proceeded to the English island fortress, Singapore, where they spent several days with British Royal Air Force (R.A.F.) pilots, many of them veterans of the Battle of Britain.

Next they boarded a third ship, a Norwegian freighter, and started up the west coast of the Malay

Peninsula. Their destination was Burma's most important city, Rangoon. It was a stifling trip. The first night
out, Rector heard a strange crackling noise. He turned
on the light. Below, hundreds of two-inch-long cock-
roaches were scuttling across the deck.

At Rangoon the volunteers were greeted by Harvey
Greenlaw, Chennault's operations officer. Most of the
volunteers had never been out of the United States before, and Rangoon was a city of fascination. But there
was no time for sightseeing. Greenlaw hurried the men
aboard a train heading north.

Rector and Hill were entranced by the passing Burmese scenery—the pagodas, the strange huts, the hordes
of workers in the fields. After traveling 170 miles, they
came to Toungoo. Since their base at Kunming, China,
was not yet completed, they would get their training
here at an abandoned R.A.F. field, Kyedaw Airdrome.

To those anticipating the mysteries and beauties of
the Far East, it was a sad disappointment. The asphalt
runway was surrounded by marshes and steaming
jungles. Rotting vegetation made the air thick with a
sour, sickening stink. The tropic heat, combined with
frequent torrents of rain, made the volunteers feel as
if they were living in a huge Turkish bath.

Their barracks were made of bamboo and teak, with
plenty of ventilation. But through the open windows
swarmed large mosquitoes and other stinging insects.

The newcomers found many old friends. Approximately half of the 110 pilots who would eventually
train at Toungoo were from the Navy. Six came from

23

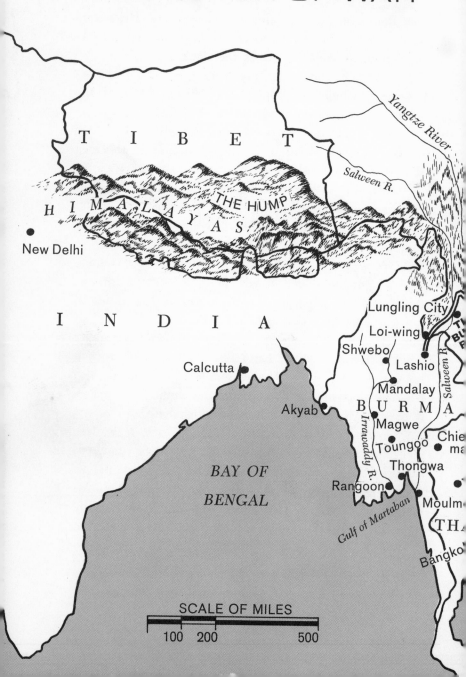

CHINA · BURMA · INDIA
THEATER OF WAR

T I B E T

Yangtze River

Salween R.

HIMALAYAS

THE HUMP

New Delhi

I N D I A

Lungling City

Loi-wing

Shwebo

Lashio

Calcutta

Mandalay

Akyab

B U R M A

Magwe

Irrawaddy R.

Salween R.

Chie
ma

Toungoo

Thongwa

BAY OF
BENGAL

Rangoon

Moulm

Gulf of Martaban

THA

Bangko

SCALE OF MILES

100   200   500

the Marine Flying Corps, and the rest were from the Army Air Forces. In spite of the bad living conditions and usual grumbling about bad food, the spirit of the men was high.

A few had enrolled merely to get out of the service. And a few had already given the American Volunteer Group (AVG) an unsavory reputation by their uncontrolled behavior in town.

On the whole, however, the AVG was a group of high-principled young men, eager for adventure. They disliked the red tape of the Army and Navy and wanted action. Many like Ed Rector had been inspired from youth by stories of war aces. They felt that the United States would never get into the war, so this was their only way to see action. Then there were a few like Tex Hill who saw that China's battle was America's.

2.

A few days after their arrival, the new detachment was taken to another building. Here for the first time they saw the man who had brought them from America. Both Hill and Rector were immediately impressed by Chennault's face and manner. Hill thought he looked like one of the strongest characters he had ever seen— the kind of man you could instantly trust. When Rector saw Chennault's hawk-like profile, and deeply lined face, he thought, "Everything I've heard about him is true."

"We have a lot of preparations to make," said Chennault. "And I want you boys to turn to. The facilities

are not much good. But you came over here to fight
—I hope." His deep-set black eyes suddenly twinkled,
and he grinned.

The day at Toungoo began at 6:00 A.M. with a lecture by Chennault in a teakwood classroom. His years
as a rural-school teacher and director of an Air Corps
flying school made him an excellent instructor. He soon
taught his students all the bitter lessons about aerial
combat that he had learned. Using captured Japanese
flying manuals, he instructed them in the enemy's
tactics.

"You will face Japanese pilots who are superbly
trained in mechanical flying," he said. "They fly by the
book and these are the books they use. Study them and
you will always be one step ahead of the enemy." The
Japanese, he said, had courage and judgment but lacked
initiative. "Bombers will hold their formations until they
are all shot down. Fighters always try the same tricks
over and over again."

Chennault showed his men how to break up the
enemy formations and make them fight according to
his style. He drew diagrams, like a football coach ex-
plaining plays, and told them exactly what to do in
every emergency.

The plane they would fly, he admitted, had many
weak points. The P-40 was so heavily armored it climbed
slowly and was sluggish in turns. But he taught them
to use the Tomahawk's great weight to advantage. It
could dive at extraordinary speed. "You can count on
a higher top speed," said Chennault, "faster dive and

Colonel Chennault discusses a mission with his men.

superior fire power. The Japanese fighters have a much faster rate of climb, higher ceiling and better maneuverability."

He warned them never to dog-fight or try to turn with a Japanese fighter. "Use your speed and diving power to make a pass, shoot and break away."

He also taught them to forget what they had learned in service schools about fighting solo or in threes. By diagrams he proved that if they fought in pairs, they would live longer. "Hit hard, break clean and get into position for another pass. Never worry about what's going to happen next, or it will happen to you."

The men listened avidly for they knew he spoke from experience. Although his great combat record in the

Chinese air force was almost unknown in America, Chennault was already a famous figure in the Orient. Here it was common knowledge that he had fought the Japanese in a Hawk 75—and had shot down more than forty planes.

In spite of this general respect, some of the pilots silently disagreed with Chennault. And there were many complaints about the Tomahawk. Among fliers, it had always had a reputation as a killer in the hands of a beginner. Already there had been two casualties at Toungoo. Jack Armstrong, a friend of Hill and Rector's at the Norfolk Naval Station, had collided during a mock fight in mid-air with another friend, Gil Bright. Bright parachuted to safety, but Armstrong went down with the two interlocked ships. Shortly after that an Army flier was caught in a monsoon and crashed into a mountain.

After the early-morning lecture, Chennault would climb up into the bamboo control tower and through field glasses watch his pupils dog-fight. He would shout instructions into a microphone while a secretary copied down comments on each pilot's technique.

Some mornings the men would go up four at a time, with one acting as a Japanese bomber. The other three would take turns attacking at all angles and levels. Other days the men would pair off and charge at each other top speed, head on.

In the individual dogfights, Rector would often let his partner, usually Christman, get on his tail so he could learn what to do when a Japanese cornered him.

29

After much practice Rector found a solution. At the top of a loop he would suddenly chop off all power and put his flaps down to further reduce speed. The man trailing him had so much speed he always flashed by and Rector would promptly get on his tail.

He passed this information on to other pilots and they in turn revealed their tricks. Though the quality of flying rapidly improved, Chennault still had much work to do. More than half of his men had never flown fighter planes before. Although the Navy dive-bombers, like Hill and Rector, soon caught on to fighter tactics, many of the bomber and transport pilots couldn't seem to get the knack of the unwieldy P-40. One transport pilot kept landing twenty feet above ground. In two months he had five American flags painted on his plane —one for each Tomahawk he had wrecked—and was dubbed the Japanese Ace.

Scarcely a week went by without a serious accident. The climax came on November 3, 1941. Seven planes were wrecked during training. Chennault was so disgusted he signaled the pilots to quit for the day. A moment later a mechanic on a bicycle raised the total to eight when he bumped into a parked plane and put it out of commission. The pilots called it "Circus Day."

By now dissatisfaction with the P-40 was becoming open. A dozen men, using this as a partial excuse, quit the AVG. Several others came to Chennault and said they were too frightened to fly in combat and asked for ground duty.

Chennault was glad to get rid of those who wanted

to leave the Group. And he listened sympathetically to those who confessed they didn't have the stomach to fight in the air. He was glad to have them as part of his ground crew.

His methods of handling men were as unorthodox as his combat tactics. He felt rigid military discipline was no solution. Only high-spirited and adventurous fliers would have responded to his call for risky service in a distant land.

He held meetings once a week and everyone with a gripe was allowed to speak up. There was no guardhouse, no long list of regulations. If there were minor infractions of the simple rules laid down in the CAMCO contracts, the offender was fined up to $100 by a board of staff officers and squadron leaders.

Uniforms were not worn. The men prided themselves on individual dress: cowboy hats and boots, Russian astrakhans, overalls, anything that proved comfortable. Chennault himself usually directed operations from his rickety tower in shorts, sports shirt and an old felt hat.

Though there was no rank and no one was required to salute, it was the rare man who didn't address Chennault as Colonel and salute. But when the work day was over and the men played baseball or volley ball, the head of the AVG was treated like anyone else. And when he acted as umpire, it was a common sight to see some mechanic screaming at him in rage when called out on strikes.

To the outsider this strange way of running a group of fighting men often seemed chaotic. All of Chen-

Chennault takes his turn at bat.

nault's problems—the unimportant gripes of the many and the real insurrection of the few—were in the open, and it was little wonder that he got the following cable from Dr. Soong:

> REPORTS TO U.S. WAR DEPARTMENT STATE YOUR GROUP CANNOT BE READY BEFORE FEBRUARY 1942 AND WILL NOT LAST TWO WEEKS IN COMBAT. YOUR COMMENT REQUESTED.

Chennault told Soong and Chiang Kai-shek his men would be ready to fight by the end of the month and would last in combat "as long as they were needed."

Chennault was plagued with another headache. Not a single trained staff officer had been sent from America to help him run the organization. He was forced to improvise a staff from men already in the Orient. The great majority of these weren't suited by training or experience for such heavy responsibilities. Consequently the smallest problems were referred to Chennault, and the most trivial decisions had to be made by him.

By a stroke of fortune the columnist Joseph Alsop, then a reserve naval officer, met Chennault at a garden party in Chungking and decided to throw in his lot with the AVG. After sending personal wires to Secretary of the Navy Knox and James Forrestal, Alsop was allowed to resign his commission and join the Group.

Alsop helped bring order from chaos at the Kunming headquarters. Then he began scouring the Far East for spare parts, tires and British .303 ammunition for those P-40s which had machine guns of this caliber.

About this time a dramatic event raised the spirits of the AVG. A number of R.A.F. pilots flew up to Toungoo in their stubby American-made Brewster Buffalos. The Americans had long been complaining that it wasn't fair for them to be flying a "no-good" plane because the best had been given to foreigners.

The British fliers kept challenging the Americans to send up their best against the R.A.F.'s best in a mock dogfight. After many refusals, Erik Shilling, who had a reputation as the Group's "hottest" pilot, was selected to represent the AVG. The two fighters took off. The

R.A.F. man, who had shot down some ten Nazis in the Battle of Britain, started to get on Shilling's tail. But before he knew it he found himself being chased. To everyone's amazement Shilling easily outmaneuvered the British pilot. Other R.A.F. men came up to do battle. With equal ease, Shilling got on their tails and "shot" them down, one by one.

This inspired the AVG pilots with confidence, and they began to have more respect for their Tomahawks. By the end of November they had discovered another great feature of their plane: no matter how steep the dive, the wings did not pull off. It was obvious their ships could take heavy battle damage. They now felt that if they fought the way Chennault had taught, they would win.

Three of the men, while looking through a British magazine, saw a picture of P-40s in Africa. Shark's teeth were painted along the edge of the engine. When the men showed the picture to Chennault, he agreed to let them use the tiger shark as the Group's symbol. In a few days Christman and other artists had painted sharks on every plane. Improving on the British model, they added a red tongue and a staring red eye behind the propeller.

By the first week of December, 1941, Chennault had accomplished the impossible. He had taken some hundred pilots and several hundred ground crew of varying talents and experience and welded them into a well-knit inspired unit. The AVG was ready, willing and able to fight.

Allen Bert Christman, former staff artist (left) for the Associated Press, painted tiger shark symbols on AVG planes like the P-40 pictured below.

Chennault organized his volunteers into three squadrons. The First, which took the name, "The Adam and Eves," was comprised mostly of Army Air Corps men. The Second, "The Panda Bears," was made up mostly of Navy fliers. The Third, "Hell's Angels," was a combination of Army and Navy pilots, plus three Marines.

The four .30-caliber wing guns and two .50s in the nose of each Tomahawk were bore-sighted. Like everything else in the AVG this was done in an original manner. Since the guns had only crude gun sights, the armorers improvised a mirror that reflected on the windshield.

War talk increased and it was evident to everyone that a showdown was soon coming. Chennault's original assignment from Chiang Kai-shek had been to protect the Burma Road and prevent Chinese cities from being bombed. The Burma Road, which zigzagged across the rugged mountains separating Burma and China, was the last supply line for military aid from the free world to Chiang Kai-shek's armies. But Chennault soon realized that this road would be useless if the city of Rangoon fell. This was the Burmese port where most of the supplies landed. He suggested that he also be given the job of assisting the British defend Rangoon. The Generalissimo approved.

Chennault's men also knew something was coming. One wrote in his diary: "Looks like a bigger fight than we thought. Guess I am really in something hot now. Well, I asked for it. Wonder how I will like it."

3.

Just before dawn on December 8, 1941, Chennault and his Chief Surgeon, Tom Gentry, were sitting in the control tower looking toward Thailand—on watch in case of a surprise Japanese air attack. The two had been doing this during the hours of dawn and dusk for the past three weeks.

After the sun rose Chennault wearily clambered down from the tower. His watch was over. As he ambled across the field, a radio man ran across the grass waving a message. Pearl Harbor had been attacked! (In Hawaii, on the other side of the International Date Line, it was still December 7, 1941.)

Chennault called his men together. "This is it," he said in a businesslike tone. To Rector he sounded as if he had known all along just what would happen. "Our order of business changes. Be ready for any eventuality." He ordered them to stand a four-plane alert. The other pilots would sit in their parked planes, always ready.

About 1,750 miles to the east, in Manila, another member of the AVG, Joseph Alsop, was talking by phone to a friend in Washington—Robert A. Lovett, Under Secretary of War for air—begging him to send immediately a box of tiny tubular coils called solenoids. The E1B solenoid was the essential animating mechanism of the .50-caliber machine gun, the Tigers' main weapon. Alsop told Lovett that the AVG was in serious danger of being forced rapidly out of action for want of a small box of these minute gadgets.

Lovett agreed to send the solenoids and Alsop ran to a taxi. Chennault had just wired ordering him to return at once to Kunming by way of Hong Kong. Alsop told the taxi driver he would give him ten dollars if they reached the airport before his plane left.

As the passenger plane was taxiing to the runway, the cab chased after it, horn honking. The plane stopped and Alsop got aboard the last commercial plane to leave Manila.

The pilots of General Douglas MacArthur's air force in the Philippines had been on the alert since dawn. But that noon at the main air base, Clark Field, all planes in the air came down for lunch. When the skies were clear of American aircraft a horde of Japanese bombers and fighters suddenly appeared overhead without warning. In a few minutes half of MacArthur's bombers were flaming wrecks. The P-40 pilots who managed to get aloft found to their amazement that the enemy planes were not the primitive crates they had been told they would meet. Nor were the Japanese pilots half-blind, bespectacled amateurs. When an American turned with a Japanese, the Zero was on his tail in a twinkling, spitting hot lead into him. The dogfighting was desperate.

A year earlier Chennault had told the War Department exactly what these Zeros could do. But this information had not been passed on to the fighter pilots in the Philippines. Now the American fighters were paying with their lives. P-40 after P-40 spun to the ground in flames.

Action
at Kunming

On that first day of war nothing happened at Toungoo. The next day there were half a dozen alerts—all false. Two days after Pearl Harbor, neighboring Thailand surrendered to the Japanese without firing a shot. Chennault decided to find out what was going on at its capital, Bangkok. He ordered Shilling, who had won the mock air duels with the R.A.F. to fly over the big port city and take pictures. Ed Rector and "Crix" Christman would escort him. Chennault told them to fly high, get their pictures and hurry home. "No fighting," he cautioned.

The three climbed to 20,000 feet and flew 500 miles,

arriving over the ancient Siamese city at noon. Twenty-six Japanese ships were unloading soldiers and cargo at the docks. One airfield was jammed with fifty fighter planes, wing to wing. Another was almost solid with as many bombers. While Shilling was snapping pictures, Rector and Christman could hardly restrain themselves from diving and strafing the helpless targets but they remembered their instructions.

When Chennault saw the pictures he was furious. With a dozen bombers he could have stopped the Japanese air offensive, obviously aimed at Rangoon and Singapore, in twenty minutes. But he didn't have a single bomber. The group scheduled to operate in co-operation with the P-40s had not yet arrived. He cabled Washington, begging them to send anything that could carry bombs. But there was no reply. Washington, apparently, had bigger problems.

Chennault would not even get replacement fighter planes for some time. Desperately needed parts, including tires, would not arrive. Replacement fighter pilots already on their way to the AVG would be detoured instead to Australia. Chennault would have to face the Japanese with what he had. Some 110 pilots had arrived but because of the dozen resignations there were now fewer than 100. Of the original 100 Tomahawks, only about 75 were fit for combat.

In addition, his pilots would have to fight in planes equipped only with commercial radios not built to stand the strain of combat. And they would be forced to fire old, unreliable ammunition.

Later that same day, Chennault got more bad news. The powerful British fleet protecting Singapore had been practically wiped out in an hour. The great ships—the battle cruiser *Repulse* and the battleship *Prince of Wales*—had been sunk by Japanese bombers and torpedo planes. The keystone of the Allied defenses in Southeast Asia was obviously doomed. And Chennault knew that all-out air action on the next most important target, Rangoon, would soon begin.

On December 12 he sent the Third Squadron, the Hell's Angels, down to Mingaladon Airdrome near Rangoon to help the R.A.F. defend the city. Six days later word came from China that Kunming was being bombed. Even though twenty-five of the pilots still at Toungoo were not yet fully trained for combat, Chennault knew he had to move at once. In half a day he transferred his combat staff, ammunition, oxygen and the First and Second Squadrons a distance of 650 miles to Kunming, China. It was the first of a series of lightning-like, long-distance mass moves that would keep the Japanese off balance for the next four years and make them think Chennault had a far larger air force.

The AVG airfield was three miles from the ancient walled city of Kunming at the north end of a 150-square-mile muddy lake. They were on a vast plateau 5,000 feet above sea level, and the cool weather was a refreshing change from the dank humidity of Burma. The new field was surrounded by rice paddies and flanked by steep, rugged peaks—the foothills of the great chain of mountains leading to the Himalayas.

Chennault felt much safer here than he had in Toungoo, where there was no real air warning system. Kunming was the headquarters of the remarkable warning net set up by the Chinese under Chennault's direction. It was a mammoth spider web of watchers equipped with radios, telephones and telegraph. The man who had organized the system according to Chennault's specifications was Colonel Wang Shu-ming, nicknamed Tiger because of his ferocity in air combat. Only five feet six inches, he was powerfully built and had a broad, good-natured face.

The system had become so effective that the inhabitants of Kunming now got at least an hour's warning before each raid. Chennault was given the most detailed information by Tiger Wang: the number of Japanese planes, their altitude and destination. At first Chennault had wondered how such details could come from ground observers, and he was dubious about the reliability of the information.

"How do you know so much?" he had asked Tiger.

"Air defense communications," was the mysterious reply.

Chennault learned not to question Tiger's information. It invariably proved to be accurate. But he had good reason to suspect Tiger hadn't told him everything. A year earlier three Japanese communications officers on reconnaissance had been shot down and captured. For months they were Tiger's personal prisoners. Regularly he would visit them, arguing about the course of the war. Never tortured or mistreated, they slowly became convinced that China, Britain and America would eventually win the war. After almost a year of this subtle brain-washing, the three men finally agreed to help the Allied cause. Tiger put them in Chinese uniforms and brought them into his office as communications experts.

As soon as Japanese bombers took off, the three willing captives decoded their countrymen's messages and within a few minutes Tiger was in Chennault's office with exact information. Several times he was tempted to tell Chennault about the source of his information. But he always decided to wait until the war was over and the three Japanese were safely home. Thus only he knew the truth. Even his own chief of staff had no suspicion that the three code experts were turncoats.

On the first day at Kunming, Chennault sent up three reconnaissance patrols. Not an enemy was in sight. The second day, December 20, dawned. Again the skies were empty of Japanese planes. Then at 9:45 A.M. a phone rang in Chennault's bare office—located in the tan, plaster headquarters building. The phone was a special one connected to the Chinese code room.

A voice at the other end said, "Ten Japanese bombers crossed the Yunnan border at Laokay heading northwest." It was Tiger Wang, who also served as the Chinese chief of staff for the AVG. Tiger added that these were twin-engine planes and had left Hanoi at 9:30 A.M. "Course northwest at 8,000 feet and climbing. Objective Kunming."

Crew chiefs relax in the "ready room" at the Flying Tigers' Kunming
air base.

Chennault hung up. A few minutes later, word came
from a spotter about 180 miles away that the Japanese
bombers had flown past—heading for Kunming. The
first alert was given. A canvas ball colored red was
raised to the top of the airport's air warning mast.
Pilots of the Adam and Eves and the Panda Bears,
lounging in the little alert shacks or the ready room of
the headquarters building, hurried into their bulky flying
suits, grabbed parachutes and hustled to their planes.

To Ed Rector it was the most exciting moment in his
life. What he had read about so often in magazines and
books would soon be happening to him. He buckled his
parachute, tightened the straps and clambered into the

cockpit of his P-40. In addition to the gleaming shark's teeth, Christman had painted a cartoon of Rector on the fuselage. The cowling that protected his motor was off, and he shouted to his crew chief to replace it.

Back in Chennault's office, reports were coming in from ground observers: "Heavy engine noise at station X-10." "Unknowns overhead at station P-8." The ten bombers were heading directly for Kunming as Tiger Wang had predicted. Chennault ordered Jack Newkirk, leader of the Panda Bears, to intercept the raiders with Christman, Gil Bright and Rector.

When Rector got his orders over the field radio, the cowling was still off his plane. He fumed when a yellow flare shot up—the signal to warm engines. Then came the red flare and the other three Panda Bears took off. At last Rector's cowling was in place. He started his engine. Just then four more Panda Bears—led by Jim Howard, whose parents had been medical missionaries

Outside their headquarters, pilots of the American Volunteer Group await instructions.

in China—took off. They were to fly over Kunming on defensive patrol.

The other planes were out of sight when Rector taxied into position. He climbed to 15,000 feet. His goggles frosted and even with the heater and heavy suit it was bitter cold. The sky was filled with great billowing clouds, and he could see the ground only occasionally. He headed east, hoping to overtake his three comrades before the battle started.

Chennault was in a car racing toward a clay pyramid overlooking the airfield. Here was the combat-operations shelter. Once inside he studied the plotting board by match light and eagerly waited for the first radio report from his pilots. It was the great moment he had been waiting years for. Soon he would know if his theories were practical. He would find out if American pilots trained in his tactics, flying American planes and aided by the Chinese warning net he had organized could stop the Japanese bombers.

He felt the fate of China was at stake and he wished he were up there with his young pilots. Suddenly the radio crackled. "Shark Fin Blue calling base." *Shark Fin* was the code for AVG, and *Blue* stood for New-kirk's flight. "Bandits sighted sixty miles east. Attacking." Then the voices of Christman and Bright broke in. The three pilots began jabbering excitedly: "There they are!" "No, no, they can't be Japs!" "Yes! Look at those red balls."

Then there was agonizing silence. Chennault figured that the Japanese bombers would probably turn and head for home as soon as Newkirk attacked. He ordered Robert ("Sandy") Sandell, leader of the Adam and Eves, to cut the bombers' line of retreat with sixteen planes.

Newkirk's flight had hesitated, like hunters with buck fever. Consequently, they had time to make only one pass. By then the Japanese had dumped their bombs, dived to get speed and were on their way back to Indochina.

Sandell's 16 planes were flying at 16,000 feet above solid overcast, some 75 miles northeast of Kunming, when they spotted the enemy. The ten Japanese planes were far below them, skimming the overcast. They were apparently lost, trying to find a way through the "soup."

A formation of P-40s, looking like a school of sharks, wings off to intercept a Japanese squadron over China.

The Adam and Eves gave chase and ten minutes later caught their prey. Forgetting everything Chennault had told them, they dived in rat-race formation, every pilot picking his own target. It was a wild melee with no teamwork. Some were trying 90-degree deflection shots, others were dog-fighting in approved World War I fashion. Their bullets sprayed all over the sky, narrowly missing each other.

Rector saw the Adam and Eves make their first pass. He gunned his motor and headed east. Like well-disciplined ducks, the enemy bombers were still flying in a big V formation, broken down into smaller Vs. Rector was above and to the left of the formation, in perfect position for a high side pass. He thought, "There they are!" He was excited, yet strangely calm. Suddenly everything was clear and obvious. He was surprised at his own coolness. He never dreamed it would be like this. As he nosed over into a steep dive, he could only think, "Why don't they fall?"

He turned and made a side pass. Getting behind a bomber, he started firing. Chennault had told him over and over again to make a short burst only. But he was so fascinated by his target he kept firing for eight seconds. Only when he was about to crash into the bomber's tail did he realize what he was doing. At the last second he shoved the stick forward and the P-40 skimmed past the other plane.

Rector was only a dozen feet away and he could see the detailed camouflage of the Japanese bomber—even its rivets. With great clarity he saw the "dust-bin" (rear) gunner slumped over, probably dead. He could also see the red winking of another gun.

He pulled out to the left and returned for another high side pass. But when he looked back, the bomber was burning like a great bonfire. Weirdly it kept flying in formation. Finally its nose dipped and it plummeted to earth.

He turned and watched Sandell's squadron continue their reckless passes. "That's the way to get killed," he thought. He remembered what Chennault had told him about the superior fire power and armor of the P-40 and what an advantage this gave in a head-on pass.

He raced past the Japanese formation, turned and headed straight for the leading bomber. The two planes approached like two gun fighters. At about 800 yards Rector pressed the trigger. One of his four .30-caliber guns went, "Pop, pop, pop." The others were silent. So were the two .50s.

He pulled back the stick and zoomed over the bomber, realizing he had forgotten to recharge his guns. He turned, went forward again and as he got into position for another head-on attack, he pumped the charger three times. Now he was in beautiful position. He pressed the trigger. There were two pops only.

Again Rector pulled up. Frustrated, he recharged the guns and made a third head-on pass. This time the guns wouldn't fire at all. He got on the high side of the bomber and charged his guns half a dozen times. But when he tested, the guns wouldn't fire at all. The first long burst had heated them to such a degree that they were stuck and refused to fire.

There was nothing to do now but go home. He didn't know the terrain and he had no navigating map, only a makeshift photographed map with no detail. He flew alongside the Japanese bombers a few minutes, then turned and headed in the exact opposite direction. This he figured, would take him back to Kunming. But he was heading to the northeast, which would cause him to miss his target by 200 miles.

By now even the impulsive tactics of the Adam and Eves were getting results. Louis Hoffman got on the tail of one Japanese bomber, slowed his speed so he would skid by, and then shot up the length of the fuselage. The plane plunged down, out of control. A second enemy bomber went down in flames after a head-on attack by Sandy Sandell.

Fritz Wolf got on the tail of one bomber and finally set its gas tanks ablaze with a burst from 100 yards. As the Japanese ship exploded, Wolf pulled into a steep climb to get away from the debris. A moment later he dived on another raider. Though he could see its rear gun winking, none of the bullets hit Wolf. He closed to fifty yards, then concentrated a long burst on one motor. The ship caught fire and exploded.

Chennault was back at the field by the time the Adam and Eves began to straggle in, swooping down in victory rolls. The pilots clustered around their chief, jabbering excitedly. At least three Japanese had been seen going down in flames. Most of the others were smoking.

"It was a good job," said Chennault, "but not good enough. Next time get them all." The pilots were brought to the operations shack where Chennault, a pipe clenched in his teeth, calmly went over every detail of the sky battle. He pointed out their mistakes. If they had followed his lessons, he said, they would have shot down all ten.

Years later they learned they had actually come near to doing that. Only one bomber returned home safely; the other wounded survivors of the fight crashed en route. Each volunteer who had a clear-cut, confirmed victory was put down for the $500 bonus promised by Chiang Kai-shek. When there was doubt, the men involved agreed, without argument, to divide the money.

In nearby Kunming the first action of the AVG was already being celebrated as a great victory. Messages of congratulations began to flow in from Chiang Kai-shek and members of his staff. Only one thing marred the day for the AVG. One of their members, Ed Rector, was missing—probably dead.

As it happened, Rector was still alive, but he was lost and running out of gas. If he didn't find an airfield soon, he would have to make a crash landing. He saw a road leading to a town. Beyond was what looked like an airfield. He dived and followed the road, but it suddenly disappeared in clouds. At an altitude of 1,000 feet he turned down a valley to keep from plunging into the surrounding hills. In a moment he realized he was trapped in a narrowing canyon. Soon the heavy overcast forced him down to 400 feet, and there was no room to circle back. It was the most harrowing moment of his life.

Suddenly the canyon turned at almost a 90-degree angle. Rector jammed his rudders, and his left wing tip seemed to scrape the rocky wall. Ahead he could see a straight stretch running on for about two miles. He knew he had to act immediately. He gave his motor full power and climbed into the overcast. He never expected to get out and wondered when he would plunge into a mountain. He climbed to 7,000 feet, and only when he saw a little light above did he at last dare to hope. Abruptly he broke into the clearest, bluest day he had ever seen. On all sides were towering peaks. It was incredible that he had come through without crashing. He made a 180-degree turn and headed back for the town. The red light on his instrument panel was shining, indicating that only a ten-minute supply of gas remained.

At last the terrain was flat. He put down his flaps to slow his speed and skimmed over a maize field to see how level it was. He turned and, as he was coming in for a landing, saw clusters of people streaming from town. He headed toward the field but didn't lower his wheels. It would be safer to make a belly landing.

When he was five feet above the field, he cut the motor and made a stall landing. He hit the furrows of the field at right angles and stopped. Looking around, Rector was completely confused. He wasn't even sure if he might not be in Japanese territory. As a crowd of people raced toward him, he pulled out his revolver.

But there were so many he decided to put away the gun. Instead he waved and called out, "*Megwa fegur.*" He had been told it meant, "American pilot." If these were Chinese, he hoped they recognized the markings on the wings. He was the first American volunteer to crash-land in China.

A moment later he was engulfed by wildly enthusiastic Chinese. One could speak English, and Rector told him how the ten Japanese bombers had been turned back.

Word of the victory spread rapidly through China. Compared to the mammoth air actions in Europe, the fight that morning had been small. But it had great significance in the Far East. For the first time, the Japanese had been turned back before bombing their target. They had been forced to dump their bombs wherever they could. A new surge of hope swept the Chinese. At last they had powerful friends and would no longer be at the mercy of Japanese bombers. Newspapers were filled with stories of the young Americans, and they were given a new name, *Fei Weing*—Flying Tigers.

This single air battle also had a great effect on the Japanese. When only one raider returned to Hanoi they were shaken. Never before had they met opposition in Kunming. Stung by this defeat they would not attack oft-bombed Kunming again for more than a year.

But they were marshaling their air forces for overwhelming attacks on another city—Rangoon.

Tigers
over Rangoon

1.

While the two squadrons of Flying Tigers at Kunming were enjoying brisk weather, their comrades of the Third Squadron, the Hell's Angels, were sweltering in the tropical heat of Rangoon. Located near the mouth of the Irrawaddy River, this sprawling, bustling city had become the only gateway to China. Its docks were piled with American lend-lease materials for Chiang Kai-shek.

Once Rangoon fell, the Japanese could sweep up the river to Mandalay and Lashio. Then the Burma Road would be useless and India itself would be wide open to attack. The Japanese plan was simple. First they would bomb Rangoon and Mingaladon Airdrome, only twelve miles away. After one or two strikes, the defending British air force of some thirty Buffalo fighters and ten Blenheim bombers would be wiped out and the city would be a helpless target. Within several weeks Rangoon would be so paralyzed that a few divisions of Japanese ground troops could seize it.

This plan took everything into consideration—except the pilots and fourteen P-40s of the Hell's Angels. Chennault had told their leader, Arvid Olson, just what to expect. He had instructed Olson to make his headquarters at Mingaladon and also to make use of a number of camouflaged emergency fields. Thus a single bombing couldn't wipe out the entire squadron. Then he told Olson he was on his own. It was up to him to defend Rangoon.

Some of the British in Rangoon were not enthusiastic about the newcomers. Several of the more high-spirited Tigers had already staged ricksha rides through the crowded streets—with Americans pulling the protesting coolies. Others had started fights when they were snubbed by waiters at exclusive clubs. A few articles in local newspapers had even labeled the American Volunteer Group as ruffians and roughnecks, and stated that their services were not wanted. The R.A.F. in their Brewster Buffalos could defend Rangoon without the help of such trash.

The day after the great victory at Kunming, the Hell's Angels saw the Japanese for the first time. A formation of twenty-seven bombers came roaring across the Gulf of Martaban, but when the raiders caught sight of the Flying Tigers patrolling the skies over Rangoon, they turned tail and headed back for Bangkok. Later that same day a single Japanese photo-reconnaissance plane flew high above Rangoon and the Mingaladon field.

The Hell's Angels remembered what Chennault had told them so often: after a photo plane comes over, a raid should be expected in one to forty-eight hours. Pilots and ground crew alike slept little that night in expectation of the coming battle. When nothing happened the next day, tension mounted.

Just after dawn on December 23, fifty-four Japanese army bombers left Bangkok and headed north. Near the border of Burma and Thailand, they were joined by twenty fighters—twelve I-97s (Nakajimas) and eight Japanese navy Zeros. The seventy-four planes split into two groups and headed west toward the shimmering Gulf of Martaban. The first wave would concentrate on Rangoon; the second on Mingaladon. Little trouble was expected.

The telephone in Olson's alert tent on the edge of Mingaladon field rang at 10:30 A.M. R.A.F. operations ordered all ships off the airdrome. There was no explanation. Guessing that the Japanese were coming, Olson passed the word to his pilots, "Scramble!"

The twenty pilots scurried across the field in a race for the fourteen planes. Ed Overend was just starting on a holiday to Rangoon by bicycle. He pedaled frantically for the nearest Tomahawk and was soon in the air. Buffalos and P-40s were roaring across the field

ly missing those pilots still afoot.
man won his race to a plane by a
taxied away with the loser's curses
Not far away, Paul Greene took off
wboy boots, shorts and a six-shooter.
clambered into his plane, a crew
at there were only 900 pounds of

for this trip," said Gilbert.
gers were still climbing, R.A.F. operations told them: "Enemy approaching from east." That
was all. They had no idea what the odds would be.

By this time the first wave of bombers were dropping
their loads on Rangoon, hindered only by several futile
anti-aircraft bursts which exploded far from the raiders.
Soon the docks were flaming. Other bombs fell among
the crowded hovels of the dock workers. As great
billows of smoke rose from ravaged Rangoon, the enemy
fighter planes suddenly swooped down on the city
streets, where the curious had gathered in crowds.
Barely skimming over the buildings, the Zeros strafed
the streets, chopping down hundreds of spectators.

Now the second wave of bombers swept over the
Gulf of Martaban, swung around the smoldering city
and headed for Mingaladon Airdrome. Above them and
several miles to the rear hovered their fighter escort—a
dozen I-97s. Specks dropped from their bellies and
some of the ground crew thought bombs were falling.
But these were auxiliary gas tanks. The fighters were
readying for combat.

Black smoke billows up over a section of the Rangoon docks.

The fourteen P-40s and sixteen of the Brewsters flung themselves at the V formation of twenty-seven twin-motored bombers. The Japanese raiders closed in for protection and opened up a deadly cross fire, filling the air with white tracers. The Americans and British didn't hesitate, diving boldly at the marauders. Neil Martin, a former Army pilot, led three mates into a right-angled attack. Bullets from at least a dozen turret guns slammed into Martin's Tomahawk. It hesitated, then plunged down into the earth and exploded. The first Flying Tiger had died in battle.

Though several bombers were already flaming, the

formation never wavered as other planes filled the key positions with well-executed crossovers. But Henry Gilbert and Paul Greene spotted several stragglers, perhaps from the first wave, and dived on them. It was a trap. From nowhere half a dozen Japanese fighters suddenly swarmed on the Americans. One bomber abruptly spun out of control, spilling out clouds of black smoke. In retaliation, four Japanese fighters stabbed at Gilbert's P-40. Its engine smoked, then the wings burst into flame. The plane dropped like a blazing comet, carrying Gilbert to his death. He had not needed a full tank of oxygen.

Greene's P-40 was also tumbling out of control. He jumped. As he floated down in his shorts and cowboy boots, two Japanese fighters attacked. But Greene yanked the cords of his parachute and his body swayed out of range. Time and again the Japanese flashed by, their .30-caliber machine guns stuttering. Each time Greene spilled the air from his chute. Suddenly he hung limply and those who had been anxiously watching from the ground thought he must be dead. So did the Japanese and they sped off.

Mechanics ran to a rice paddy to recover Greene's body. Although the chute was peppered with bullet holes, Greene was untouched. "I just got tired," he said, "and couldn't spill my chute any more."

Bombs, meanwhile, were falling on Mingaladon. One hit the operations building. Another blasted a hangar, wiping out a British ground crew. In a few minutes the runways were torn up and gaping craters pocked the entire field. Following the same pattern used at Clark Field in the Philippines, Japanese fighters now plummeted down and raked the parked planes. Eight R.A.F. trainers burst into flames.

The Flying Tigers pursued the bombers over the Gulf of Martaban. Finally all reluctantly broke off the fight and returned—except Duke Hedman. A farm boy from South Dakota, he had always been the most conservative pilot in the Group. He was so cautious in training that the other Tigers secretly thought he would never stand a chance in battle. That morning he had been the last to get off the ground—as usual. But when he got his first glimpse of Japanese fighters, he abandoned his cautious ways and slashed into attack with reckless abandon. He knocked down one I-97 on his first dive, then pulled up behind a bomber. Before it spun out of formation, its gunners had smashed Hedman's canopy.

In spite of this, he climbed and made another dive at the fighters. Two dropped out of the fight, probable kills, but other I-97s got on his tail. They hit Hedman's gas tank several times and picked off his gun sights.

But Duke Hedman was not through. He was still chasing the invaders over the Gulf. Near the border of Thailand he flew into the middle of the formation and sent another bomber down in flames. Then, at last, he returned home.

No one will ever know how many planes the Hell's Angels shot down that day. Though the pilots claimed fifteen, Squadron Leader Olson radioed Chennault that only six were confirmed victories. But R.A.F. searching parties found thirty-two wrecked Japanese planes around Rangoon, and the British pilots claimed only seven.

Great as the victory was, two pilots of the Hell's Angels were dead. Nor was this the end of the day's bad news for the squadron. Three other Hell's Angels crashed into a mountain while ferrying new pursuit planes back to Kunming. Two narrowly escaped death, but the third was killed.

It was obvious that more and heavier Japanese raids were coming, and Olson now had only twelve planes and fifteen available pilots.

2.

The day before Christmas dawned hot and muggy. The temperature rose to 115 degrees. In nearby Rangoon gallant British volunteers had put out the fires and cleared the streets. But looters were roaming the damaged areas. The roads to the north and west were jammed with refugees; the coolies and workers had no bomb shelters and refused to go through another terror bombing.

In the mass flight, the Tigers had lost their servants and food. They breakfasted on stale bread and then spent the quiet day reviewing their first fight. New tactics were planned. They would separate the enemy fighters and bombers. They had learned that if a Japanese fighter was delayed even for a few minutes, he didn't have the speed to catch up with the bombers.

The P-40s, however, with their superior diving speed, could catch the bombers.

On Christmas morning Radio Tokyo boasted of great victories all over Southeast Asia. Then the announcer promised the people of Rangoon "a bundle of Christmas presents."

As the morning wore on and no reports came from the British warning system, Olson became nervous and ordered George McMillan to take up a three-plane reconnaissance patrol. A little after 11:00 A.M. the phone in Olson's alert tent rang. The R.A.F. reported: "Japs on the way." At almost the same moment McMillan radioed: "Great Jap bomber force on the way sixty miles out."

Olson ordered the remaining nine P-40s into the air. As Duke Hedman climbed into his battered plane, a mechanic told him the gas tank still had holes and the gun sight hadn't been replaced. "I never use a gun sight anyway," he said and took off.

At 12:05 P.M. the Tigers, who had climbed to 20,000 feet, were warned that the enemy "was expected over in ten minutes." They sped east and when they reached Thongwa at 12:15 P.M. saw a terrifying flotilla of planes surging toward them. At the field, Olson later counted sixty bombers and eighteen fighters. But some of those aloft insist to this day that there were three waves of attackers—seventy-one bombers and forty-two fighters.

Twelve P-40s and sixteen clumsy Brewsters flew out to meet this mighty force.

"It's like rowboats attacking the Spanish armada!" said

Following an air-raid alarm, squadron leader George B. McMillan scans the skies for Japanese raiders.

one awed ground observer.

By this time the twelve P-40s had split into two flights of six—one group led by McMillan and one by Parker Dupuoy. McMillan's flight reached the first wave of enemy planes before it got to Rangoon. McMillan and R. T. ("Tadpole") Smith dived into the bomber formation, while Hedman and three others engaged the fighter escort. McMillan downed two bombers. Then, over the Gulf, he got up to within ten feet of another bomber and fired. As the invading aircraft burst into flames, two of its cannon shells tore into the P-40. McMillan dived, his motor spewing smoke. He glided, wheels up, into a rice paddy.

Duke Hedman, meanwhile, had shot down two I-97 fighters and was chasing another. But four other Nakajimas swooped down. Hedman's canopy flew off. He stooped over the stick as the wind swept past his head, and dived steeply. The Japanese pilot, seeing him bent over, probably imagined him dead. Anyhow he went after a new target. When Hedman landed at a satellite field, guns empty as usual, mechanics asked him how many bandits he had knocked down this time.

He didn't know. "It's bad luck to count 'em," he said. In the coming months he would shoot down more planes but never again claim another one.

Meanwhile, two other pilots in McMillan's flight, Charlie Older and Tom Haywood, acting as a team, were knocking down bomber after bomber. Though all the main spars from Haywood's left wing had been shot away, the two continued until five Japanese had been destroyed.

The other flight of six Tigers, led by Parker Dupuoy, boldly attacked the third wave—twenty-seven bombers escorted by Zero fighters. Dupuoy quickly shot down one Zero; his wingman got another.

Two of his men had just heard a radio order, "Pancake immediately." Obediently they headed for the field, not realizing an English-speaking Japanese had given the order. As they were letting their wheels down, half a dozen Japanese fighters swept onto their tails, ripping them with bullets. The two Tigers yanked back their sticks and zoomed up. But by then the fight had drifted out of sight. And Dupuoy's flight was reduced to four.

One of these, Eddie Overend, was going after the bombers. His first burst slammed into a bomber's engines. It caught fire. Overend followed, still shooting until the bomber's wing crumpled and fell off. He climbed for another attack. After three passes he heard something like hard rainfall hitting his ship. A Zero was on his tail. He tried to pull away, but his controls were jammed and he could only go forward in a flat dive.

He hunched down and gave his engine full speed. Remembering how the Japanese had tried to kill Paul Greene, he decided not to bail out. Besides, every Tomahawk was needed badly. With wheels up he eased his ship down gently into a shallow swamp. As he started to crawl out, a group of natives ran at him shouting and waving knives and sickles. But when they saw Overend was not a Japanese, they smiled. So did Overend.

Dupuoy and his remaining two men were chasing the Japanese over the Gulf. Dupuoy dived at a Zero. The planes collided. The Zero toppled, one wing completely severed. Four feet of Dupuoy's right wing were chopped off, but he babied the P-40 back to the field and landed it safely at 140 miles an hour.

Ten of the twelve Flying Tigers who took part in the savage battle returned to Mingaladon. The fuselages and tails of their ships were filled with holes. Mechanics and armorers greeted them with wild shouts. It had been a great victory. The air battle had turned into a rout of the Japanese. The sixteen Brewsters had stopped the first wave before they could bomb the field. Eight or nine bombers had been downed—at the cost of five R.A.F. pilots.

The AVG had done much better. Olson radioed Chennault:

LIKE SHOOTING DUCKS. WOULD PUT ENTIRE JAP FORCE OUT OF COMMISSION WITH GROUP HERE.

Officially the Flying Tigers were credited with ten fighters and nine bombers, but War Correspondent Leland Stowe estimated they had knocked down at least twenty-eight Japanese. In any case the British still remaining in Rangoon were now loudly praising the Americans and putting up signs, "Welcome AVG." A week earlier the Tigers had been "ruffians." Now they were heroes.

That night a broadcast from Radio Tokyo proved that the claims of the Tigers had been far from exaggerated. The announcer called the AVG unprincipled bandits. "If they do not cease their unorthodox tactics at once," he said, "they will be treated as guerrillas."

The victory at Rangoon was the only cheering note in a day of tremendous Allied losses. MacArthur's forces in the Philippines were being hemmed into Bataan Peninsula and Hong Kong had at last fallen. With the surrender of this great British bastion, the AVG lost another man. Joseph Alsop—whose seat on the last plane to leave Hong Kong had been taken by a dog belonging to a Chinese banker's wife—was among the thousands captured.

3.

A few days later Chennault realized that the Hell's Angels were nearing exhaustion and ordered the Panda Bears to start for Rangoon. At 10:00 A.M., December 30, seventeen P-40s of the Second Squadron began to land at Mingaladon. Some half-dozen other pilots, including Ed Rector, were en route by transport plane and train.

The leader of the Panda Bears was Jack Newkirk. A Navy flier from the carrier *Yorktown*, Newkirk was tall, hawk-faced, sharp-eyed, and affected a small mustache. He was also an impetuous young man, filled with nervous energy. Frustrated by his first brief clash with the Japanese at Kunming, he longed to get into action. After a few days of quiet at Mingaladon, he decided to look for trouble. On the morning of January 3 he led Jim Howard, Bert Christman and Tex Hill on a raid into Thailand. Their target was the Japanese air base at Tak, only 170 miles east of Rangoon.

Christman had engine trouble and turned back, but the other three continued over the matted green jungle. Their maps were so poor, they were navigating by dead reckoning and had to fly at 10,000 feet to recognize the terrain. When they reached the Tak field they saw rows of bombers lined up neatly. They thought the

Japanese had been caught napping. But six army Type-96 fighters were far above them, waiting.

The three Tigers dived. As Hill was making his first pass on the parked planes, he noticed a Japanese pouring a stream of lead into Howard's tail. Hill pulled up, getting behind the Japanese. He pressed the trigger and the enemy fighter burst into flame. Suddenly Hill heard a staccato burst, and holes appeared in his own fuselage. Still unwounded, he pulled around and came

Jim Howard at Toungoo

face to face with another attacker. Hill welcomed this head-on clash, for he knew he had more fire power and stronger armor. He fired a burst and had his second victory.

Newkirk had also shot down two of the enemy planes. The last two Japanese Type-96s climbed to safety.

After all three Tiger pilots had finally landed safely at Mingaladon, Hill walked up to Howard and told him he was lucky to get back with so many holes in his tail.

Howard, who was extremely serious and deliberate, said slowly, "You're kidding."

"Let's go over and take a look."

The two walked to the rear of Howard's plane. Only when he counted eleven holes did Howard realize that, while he was methodically burning up four or five parked planes, he too had been a target.

The next morning, Sunday, Newkirk got his wish for more action. The Japanese renewed their attacks. This time twenty-seven fighters came to wipe out the AVG. There was a bitter, brief battle of fifteen minutes. Three Tigers and three Japanese were downed that day. It was the first and last time the Tigers would ever fight a draw.

The new air offensive resumed the next morning. The Japanese thought they had already knocked out the Tigers, and sent three waves of bombers to converge on Rangoon. Newkirk's men rose to meet the attack. "Like David taking after several Goliaths," a British spectator wrote in his diary.

In spite of the overwhelming odds, the Tigers and the

few remaining R.A.F. pilots beat back the attack. The next day the Japanese returned with more bombers and fighters—and were again thrown back with heavy losses.

That night the invaders tried a new trick. They sent over a small group of bombers to raid the area near Mingaladon. The main purpose was to keep ground crew and pilots awake. These day-and-night attacks went on for five days until the Tigers lost track of time and were groggy. The ground crew as well as pilots were at the edge of exhaustion. They worked on a twenty-four-hour schedule, gassing, arming and repairing the deteriorating P-40s. Radio detector crews stayed at their posts, sleeping in shifts. Never once was the AVG caught on the ground.

On the morning of January 6, 1942, Ed Rector was patrolling when he got word that seven Japanese bombers were trying to sneak into Rangoon. He raced back toward Mingaladon and saw three of them preparing to bomb the field. He made a high side-angle pass and set one bomber afire. To Rector's amazement, it stayed in formation and dropped its bombs; then it tumbled to earth. A little later he downed another enemy plane—an I-97.

The following morning there was no alert, and the afternoon was quiet too. The great five-day offensive was over. The daylight bombings had proved too costly to the Japanese. It was another spectacular victory for Chennault's men. Half a dozen P-40s had been destroyed, but not a pilot had been lost. Some thirty wrecked Japanese planes were found near Rangoon and

A P-40 combat crew cleans one of its guns between missions.

at least that many more lay at the bottom of the Gulf of Martaban or in the jungles.

The night bombings continued, however, and unfortunately the Tigers were not trained or equipped as night fighters. One attempt at night fighting ended in tragedy when a P-40 pilot tried to land in the dark and crashed into a parked car, killing a sleeping comrade.

The Flying Tigers were becoming a legend in Rangoon. Lieutenant George Graham of His Majesty's Forces visited a friend in the AVG who was using one of the satellite fields. The Tiger was shaving when the alert sounded. "I'll be back in twenty minutes," he told

Graham. Clad only in a towel, his face bearded with shaving cream, the pilot jumped into his plane, taxied down a highway and went into battle. He downed three Japanese and was back in a few minutes. "Now," he complained to Graham, "my soap is dry."

Another story going the rounds concerned Alex ("Mickey") Mihalko, communications chief of the Panda Bears. He had concocted his own enemy warning system. In the first raids, the British often neglected to let the AVG know the Japanese were coming. They would warn only their own pilots.

Mihalko began hanging around the R.A.F. radio and telephone office. When the phone rang he would obligingly pick it up. If he heard a message announcing enemy planes, he would hand the phone to an R.A.F. operator. Then he would call into the microphone beamed to all planes, "Go get 'em, cowboys!"

The British had no idea what Mihalko was talking about, but the Tigers got the message. They would take off immediately and usually beat the R.A.F. pilots into the air.

Mihalko and the rest of the ground crew were living just as dangerously as the pilots. From slit trenches they fought Japanese strafers with Tommy guns, and then ran into the open to repair the battered Tomahawks. Four mobile servicing units were organized. The moment a P-40 landed, the trucks rolled up and a dozen men began loading guns, gassing the tanks, repairing, and replenishing oxygen. In minutes the P-40 would be taxiing for take-off, while the mechanics ran back to their slit trenches.

The ground crew and administrative personnel also spent every spare moment on the Rangoon docks, loading trucks with the lend-lease equipment so sorely needed in China. Even the chaplain, Paul Frillman, worked week after week like a coolie in the oppressive heat. Each day that the Tigers managed to hold off the fall of Rangoon, another 700 tons of equipment for China started north by river barge, train, truck or plane.

4.

For more than two weeks there were no day bombings. But according to British Intelligence reports, 300 Japanese planes—180 bombers and 120 fighters—had been gathered for a final, overwhelming daylight air offensive against Rangoon. Chennault, guessing this would happen, had already sent eight pilots of the Adam and Eves to reinforce the Panda Bears.

Early in the morning of January 23, twenty-three I-97 fighters approached Mingaladon field. Their mission was to get the Tigers into the air and engage them until their fuel was gone. While the ground crews were refueling the P-40s, a wave of Japanese bombers would knock Mingaladon out of existence.

A flight of Hurricanes, reinforcements for the R.A.F., were just landing. They were almost out of gas and would be perfect targets. Tex Hill was lounging in one of the shacks when the air-raid alarm finally sounded. A radio operator ran up to him. "Two planes are ready

Frank Lawlor

to go, Tex!"

Hill and Frank Lawlor hurried onto the field. One was tall and lanky; the other short and stocky. Hill liked working with Lawlor, who was cold as ice in combat and a dead shot. They climbed and then dived into the middle of the Japanese fighter formation. The invaders started whirling in tight circles. Hill got on the tail of the nearest plane and shot it down. Then he and Lawlor got behind two other I-97s. A moment later Hill had his second victory of the day. Lawlor missed with his first burst, but he kept coming in until the Nakajima flew into pieces.

For ten minutes the two lone Tigers held off the entire attack. Finally five R.A.F. pilots joined the battle, then three more Americans. The surviving Nakajimas scattered and fled across the Gulf.

The defenders landed, grabbed a quick lunch and were back in the air in time to meet the thirty-one bombers that had expected no opposition. Flying above and to the rear was an escort of some thirty fighters.

Newkirk and nine other Tigers reached their ceiling, then dived on the first wave of bombers, each man picking a target. Coming from three directions, the Tigers made a quick pass and climbed for a second attack. Newkirk's target fell out of formation, staggered back into position. Another bomber began to smoke and flame, then dropped. Newkirk fired another burst and his victim tumbled down.

At that moment several I-97s attacked the leader of the Panda Bears. One slid past and, as he turned to climb, Newkirk caught him. A single burst blew off one wing. When Newkirk came in for a landing his flaps were blasted away and he overshot the field, nosing over at the end of the runway. He climbed out and grinned at the anxious ground-crew men who ran over to help. "I just made a thousand dollars, boys," he said.

He got into another P-40 and soon knocked down another bomber and fighter to make an additional $1,000.

Ed Rector and his partner, Crix Christman, were among the first in their planes that afternoon. While their motors were warming, Rector, who was to be wingman that day, heard the radio report, "Many bandits northeast." He pointed to his headset. Christman shook his head. His radio was dead. He motioned Rector to take the lead. He would fly wing.

The two friends climbed to 15,000 feet. About forty miles from the field they saw twenty-seven dive bombers, two-place monoplanes with rear gunners. They were just below in tight formation in two Vs. A moment later Rector saw a crowd of Nakajima fighters to the rear. He wondered when the Japanese would learn to put the fighters ahead of the bombers.

Rector called back to Mingaladon, reporting the enemy. Then he waggled his wings as a signal to Christman and the two dived at the rear of one V. Rector's pass was so fast he aimed at the whole formation and slid across the top. He pulled up, checked the oncoming fighters and decided he would have time to make one more pass at the dive bombers before the fighters arrived. He made a second pass and knocked down a bomber. He pulled out and saw Christman turning to come in for an attack. By now the enemy fighters were almost on them. Rector headed directly at them, bulling his way through the first group of fanning Nakajimas and taking snap shots.

Right behind was Christman. Soon they were engulfed by Nakajimas. Christman's motor was hit and he jumped out. As his chute burst open, a Japanese darted in and fired. One bullet penetrated the base of his skull.

The next morning every Tiger wanted to avenge the death of the popular cartoonist. The chance soon came. Bob Neale, who had brought down two Japanese the day before, saw seven single-engine bombers heading in to bomb Mingaladon. As he and Tex Hill started to dive, two stubby Brewster Buffalos hit the Japanese formation from above. One bomber blew up and the other invaders turned back in single file.

To Neale they looked like moving targets in a shooting gallery. The two Tigers bored in. Neale got the last plane; Hill picked off another. One of the R.A.F. pilots got a third. Suddenly the leading bomber, which hadn't even been attacked, blew up. The four Allied fliers now ganged up on the last two Japanese, who were soon spinning down in flames.

In two days the Panda Bears had destroyed some thirty-five planes; the R.A.F. had accounted for approximately eight others. But the Tigers could not forget Christman's death. They were in no mood for celebrating.

The Japanese attacks continued, and the Panda Bears went on knocking them down. But in the next week two more pilots were killed. By now the entire squadron—pilots and ground crew alike—were haggard and gaunt. Many hadn't had time to shave for weeks. The P-40s were in even worse condition. Only six could fly and all of these wore many patches. Only five pilots were fit for combat.

But the victories of the Flying Tigers were being celebrated all over the Allied world. Prime Minister Winston Churchill expressed the feeling of the British Empire in his cable to the Governor of Burma:

THE MAGNIFICENT VICTORIES THEY HAVE WON IN THE AIR OVER THE PADDY FIELDS OF BURMA MAY WELL PROVE COMPARABLE IN CHARACTER, IF NOT IN SCALE, WITH THOSE WON OVER THE ORCHARDS AND HOP FIELDS OF KENT IN THE BATTLE OF BRITAIN.

5.

By late January, 1942, the Adam and Eves had taken over the defense of Rangoon with the help of the surviving Panda Bears and a handful of R.A.F. fliers. Japanese ground forces were grinding relentlessly into Burma and early in February the key city of Moulmein, just across the Gulf of Martaban, fell. It was now the dry season and only one formidable barrier lay between the invaders and Rangoon—the Salween River.

The situation was so desperate the Tigers were thrown into the battle against the ground troops. They strafed infantry, assault boats and even artillery positions. Together with the R.A.F. Hurricanes, which were proving no match for Japanese fighter planes, they escorted ponderous British Blenheim bombers in attacks on the front lines.

But their main mission was still to repel air invaders. Like the Hell's Angels and Panda Bears, the Adam and Eves were learning by experience what Chennault had tried to teach them at Toungoo. In his first encounter Gregory Boyington—a short, squat former Marine flier with powerful arms and shoulders—was closing in behind two I-97 fighters. One of the Japanese planes pulled up sharply and looped above him. Boyington stopped firing and decided to turn, thinking this would prevent the Nakajima from getting on his tail. In practice he had outturned the best American pilots by tightening his neck muscles and retarding the flow of blood from his head.

Gregory Boyington

Forgetting what Chennault had said repeatedly, Boyington pulled the stick back and turned with all his strength. Though he contracted his neck muscles tightly, he blacked out momentarily. Finally he saw that the tracers were coming closer. He dived, realizing that all the tactics and close formation he had been taught in the States were useless in real combat.

He climbed 1,000 feet above the I-97. This time he made a much faster pass. He watched his tracers fly on both sides of the Nakajima. Suddenly the Japanese pilot went into one of the most remarkable acrobatic maneuvers Boyington had ever seen. And once more Boyington found himself turning with the Japanese. Later he reasoned it was only pride and ego that forced him to try a second time. But he again learned that this was the way to suicide, and dived to safety.

Sandy Sandell, the leader of the squadron, was also learning fast in combat. In his first week, he knocked down five Japanese. Moments after he had become an ace, he charged head on at a bomber. But its nose gunner hit the cooling system of Sandell's ship, forcing him to retire from the battle.

His men worshiped him. Yet a few weeks earlier in Kunming they had all signed a petition asking for a new leader. They thought Sandy was too strict. He didn't believe in pilots socializing with the ground crew and wouldn't even let them play cards together in the alert shacks.

When the petition was brought to Sandell, he read it carefully. Without saying a word, he added his signature to the long list. Then he went into the office of Chennault's assistant, Harvey Greenlaw. "Maybe they'll be better off with someone else," he said, recommending Bob Neale.

But his men never turned in the petition to Chennault. They tore it up.

Early on the morning of February 7, Sandell took up a P-40 with a new tail assembly. He wanted to test it before anybody flew it into combat. Mechanics watched anxiously as Sandell put the repaired ship through rigid acrobatics. Then he disappeared in the haze. All at once the Tomahawk came plunging into sight. At about 2,500 feet Sandell leveled off and began flipping in a series of slow rolls. Abruptly the ship went into an inverted stall and began a deadly spin. It crashed and only the tail wheel and right wheel could be salvaged.

Neale, a Navy pilot, assumed command of the Adam and Eves. Until now he had been so happy-go-lucky that some of the men had wondered what kind of leader he would be. He took over as if born to command, never asking his men to do anything he wouldn't. It was a rare mission he didn't lead. He became so aggressive that he left a fight only when he ran out of fuel or was shot out of action.

On February 15 Singapore surrendered and the elite Japanese air squadrons which had helped conquer that British stronghold were now flung into the battle for Rangoon. For the first time the Tigers ran into Zero fighters and bombers in force. The veterans of the Singapore campaign were also older and more experienced than any yet encountered by the Tigers.

Even so, Neale and his men continued to pile up victories with Chennault's tactics. But their planes were almost unflyable. Tires were chewed up, and frequently they blew out. Battery plates were so thin that when recharged they wore out in a day. There was no Prestone oil coolant, and oxygen was running low.

The dust at Mingaladon constantly fouled up the P-40 engines, clogging the carburetors so much that it had become dangerous to strafe or dog-fight. Any moment the engine might quit. Only the extraordinary skill and courage of the ground crews kept the P-40s aloft. In spite of constant bombings, strafings and the lack of replacement equipment, Chennault's mechanics kept at least ten planes in fighting condition every day.

Robert Neale

Squadron leader Bob Neale makes his flight report at a Burmese airdrome.

In contrast the R.A.F. maintenance men allowed the squadron of thirty Hurricanes which had arrived in January to dwindle to eleven by the middle of February.

In Rangoon jungle law ruled. Criminals, lunatics and lepers—loosed by British authorities—roamed the streets, trying to find food. Looters made the night more dangerous than the continued bombings. Muggings, knifings and murders became common. The Burmese, their long hatred of the British boiling over, attacked their former masters. Several times Flying Tigers coming back from the docks with loads of ammunition and weapons had to shoot their way through rioting crowds.

The docks were still piled high with American lend-lease food, automobile parts, medical supplies, machine guns and other supplies. The ground crews and staff personnel were still spending every available moment loading trucks for China.

By February 19 the Japanese army had crossed the Salween and was only seventy-five miles from Rangoon. The British commander in Burma ordered his exhausted, almost disorganized troops to "fight to the last cartridge and to the last man."

Chennault, realizing the ground situation was hopeless, radioed Neale to cease the bombing escort and strafing missions. The ramshackle P-40s should be conserved. Those planes that needed repair were to be flown to Kunming or shipped by rail. And so by twos and threes, Neale's squadron headed north. Most of the ground crew and administrative personnel left in a large truck convoy.

By February 23 Neale had only eleven planes and pilots at Mingaladon. He radioed Chennault and asked when he should leave. The reply was simple:

EXPEND EQUIPMENT. CONSERVE PERSONNEL UTMOST. RETIRE WITH LAST BOTTLE OXYGEN.

Two days later there was an air-raid warning. Neale and six other Tigers took off. When Neale realized it was a false alarm he decided to head east and strafe Moulmein. As they swept in low, three Japanese were just leaving the runway. Neale and three mates dived, knocking down two. Then they headed for a group of parked planes—so many they couldn't count them.

At that moment seven Japanese fighters on patrol struck. The Tigers fought them off, destroying at least two, and streaked for home.

That afternoon approximately forty Japanese fighters and several bombers approached Rangoon for the first daylight raid since early February. Nine Tigers and six Hurricanes tore into the swarm of invaders. Soon the sky was a raging battlefield. Japanese planes blew up like bursts of anti-aircraft shells. In less than half an hour the Tigers had thirteen more confirmed victories.

The next day about 200 Japanese planes returned in wave after wave. Half a dozen P-40s and several Hurricanes fought them off, with the Tigers bagging eighteen more fighters. In two days they had destroyed forty-three without a loss.

That night more than twenty-five blocks of Rangoon

were burning wildly. Animals released from the zoo prowled the streets. Hospitals overflowed with wounded. Other victims of the bombings lay dying in the streets as crowds of crazed natives fought the few remaining police. Wharves, mills, oil dumps and ships were in flames. Dense black clouds of smoke shut out the stars. The stench of dead bodies and burning buildings was overpowering. Rangoon itself was dying.

Neale ordered all but five pilots to start north by truck. He radioed Chennault that he was staying at Mingaladon in the hope that Ed Liebolt, who had bailed out over the jungle the day before, would show up.

On February 27 the R.A.F. took out the radar warning set at Mingaladon. Neale talked over the situation with his pilots, and they all agreed they couldn't stay at Rangoon any longer. Early the next morning four pilots took off and patrolled the AVG truck convoy moving slowly up toward China. Neale and another man made another last futile search for their missing comrade, Liebolt (who, in fact, was already dead), then reluctantly headed north.

The sixty-eight-day air battle for Rangoon was over.

Revolt
of the Tigers

1.

A few days before the Flying Tigers left Rangoon, Lieutenant General Joseph Stilwell landed at Karachi, India. President Roosevelt had sent him to help the British and Chinese stop the Japanese advance into Burma. General Stilwell had previously served in China, and he could speak some Chinese. He was a gaunt, tough field soldier who loved best to command troops under fire. Outspoken, blunt and acid-tongued, he had long since won the nickname, "Vinegar Joe."

At first Stilwell and Chiang Kai-shek got along well, and the Chinese leader agreed to let the American general have two armies to help stop the relentless Japanese drive. Stilwell's first conference with Chennault on March 2 in Kunming was also friendly. Stilwell, knowing Chennault's reputation back in Washington as a "prima donna," was agreeably surprised when the leader of the Flying Tigers readily consented to serve under him.

Two days later the Japanese took Rangoon and began to push up the Irrawaddy valley toward Toungoo, the old training ground of the Tigers. This field was now used as a refueling point for the Flying Tigers, but their main advance units were farther north at Magwe, some 250 miles from Rangoon.

Here at an unfinished airfield their ground crew hastily mended the battered P-40s. It was obvious the

General Joseph W. Stilwell (right) with Generalissimo and Madame Chiang Kai-shek after one of their first meetings.

Japanese air force would soon attack, but for almost two weeks there was an ominous quiet. Then on March 19 two Tigers—Bill Reed and Ken Jernstedt—flew on a reconnaissance mission below Rangoon. At dawn they neared the airfield at Moulmein. The ground below was completely covered by a solid white cloud bank, but the two Tigers decided—"just for fun"—to detour and take a look through a hole in the overcast.

They discovered, down below, a satellite field with twenty or thirty Nakajima fighters being gassed for some mission. The two P-40s dived, their guns ripping tracers into the neat rows of planes. The attack was such a surprise that Reed and Jernstedt made six passes without a shot being fired at them. They counted fifteen fires burning as they headed for the main field. Here they strafed a line of bombers, setting three afire. As a last insulting gesture, Jernstedt blew up a big twin-engined transport.

The next day the R.A.F. survivors of Rangoon, also stationed at Magwe, attacked their old airdrome, Mingaladon. Their low-level bombing and strafing also caught the Japanese sleeping. Sixteen planes were destroyed on the ground. And when Zero fighters finally got into the air twelve were shot down.

These twin defeats infuriated the Japanese. The following noon, March 21, twenty-seven bombers escorted by twenty Zero fighters approached Magwe. Since the R.A.F.'s one radar set covered only the southeastern approaches and there was no ground-observer net to the west, the air-raid warning didn't sound until the last moment. Only two P-40s and two Hurricanes got into the air. They shot down four Japanese, but the main force of bombers made two or three deliberate runs over the field before dropping their loads with deadly accuracy. Then Zero fighter pilots strafed planes and ground crew, even tossing out hand grenades.

In a few minutes the field was an inferno. Every Blenheim bomber was ablaze, their bomb cargoes exploding with awesome roars. Six parked Hurricanes and one P-40 were also in flames.

As soon as Chennault learned of the disastrous raid, he radioed:

LOOK OUT FOR FOLLOW-UP RAID TOMORROW.

The Americans were ready, but once more the British warning system broke down. At 8:00 A.M., as Chennault predicted, the Japanese struck again. This time not an Allied fighter got into the air. And not a Japanese plane was shot down.

When the invaders finally headed back south, the Magwe field was a total wreck and the AVG had lost two men—a pilot and a crew chief. Only three P-40s and four Hurricanes could fly. The pitiful remnants of the R.A.F. hurried west to Akyab on the Bay of Bengal. The AVG fled north by truck, train and plane to Loiwing, China, near the Burma border.

That night the Japanese announced that the "American guerrilla pilots" had all been shot down and the AVG was dead.

2.

Chennault was in bed in Kunming with an attack of chronic bronchitis when he learned the bad news. He got up to plan a revenge mission. He was sure the planes which had bombed Magwe had come from Chiengmai, a field in the teak forests of northern Thailand. So he ordered a counterattack on Chiengmai. Newkirk would lead one flight of four and Neale a flight of six.

By this time Newkirk was famed throughout America as "Scarsdale Jack." Few of his comrades, however, even knew he came from Scarsdale. His most common nickname among the Tigers was "Newquack." Ordinarily he was high-spirited and gay, but on the evening after he got the orders to raid Chiengmai he was *strangely* somber.

He told George ("Pappy") Paxton, "You can't last through the war at this pace," and offered Paxton all his whipcord cloth for a new uniform, saying, "I don't think *I'm* going to need it." Then he sought out Tex Hill and said he had a premonition about the mission.

"If I felt that way," said Hill, "I wouldn't go."

But Newkirk shook his head. He went to his room and wrote a letter to Chennault. In the event of his death he wanted his friends to have his personal effects, and he asked that Hill be given command of the Panda Bears. Then he found Chaplain Frillman and changed his will, providing for the wife he had married the week before he sailed for China.

The next morning, March 23, the revenge mission left Kunming. The ten P-40s landed at Loi-wing for gas. They waited until late afternoon and then headed for advance fields near the Thailand border.

They landed at dusk, refueled and slept under the wings of their planes. At 4:00 A.M. they were awakened. As they started to brush their teeth in an R.A.F. washroom, a British sergeant said, "Don't use that water, it's polluted!"

All but Newkirk put away their toothbrushes. He said, "A few bugs won't bother me," and brushed his teeth in the muddy water. "After tomorrow," he told one of his mates, "I don't think it'll make any difference."

The two flights took off a few minutes later. Neale's six planes were to hit the main field at Chiengmai. Newkirk's four planes were to harass a nearby satellite field to prevent Japanese fighters from attacking Neale.

Newkirk found the satellite field empty. As he started toward Chiengmai to join Neale, he noticed a truck convoy. He strafed the trucks, then dived on an armored car, followed by Hank Geselbracht, his wingman. Suddenly Geselbracht saw Newkirk's plane swerve and crash into the road. The famed Flying Tiger's premonition had come true.

In the meantime, Neale's flight had headed over the mountains and jungles with no running lights. Only their exhaust flames were visible. Ed Rector and William ("Black Mac") McGarry were flying cover above the other four planes. In the first faint, hazy light of day,

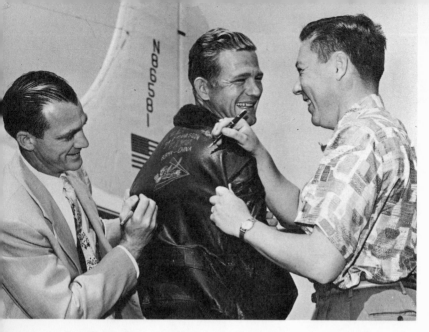

At a Flying Tiger reunion in 1952, Cliff Groh (center) puts on his old AVG jacket while Hank Geselbracht (left) and Duke Hedman (right) prepare to autograph it.

they could see little below them.

Their leader lost his way but, just as Neale was about to turn back, Charlie Bond recognized a round hill. He waggled his wings, and the others began to follow him to the left.

Finally Rector saw many tiny glares. He knew it was Chiengmai field. The Japanese must be warming up their engines. Neale and the other three pilots who were to attack tipped over and dived steeply. The four Tigers roared up and down the rows of planes, setting them on fire.

Rector watched them make about five passes in the

dim light. Some twenty Japanese planes were in flames. Blurred figures were darting from the planes like ants. Rector decided to join the attack. He shoved his stick forward and dived with McGarry not far behind. The pair made two passes.

At last radio silence was broken as someone shouted, "Let's get out of here!" The six P-40s began to pull away one by one and start for home.

It was only then that Rector noticed McGarry's plane was smoking. Neale noticed it also, and the two rode formation as their comrade headed toward a mountain. But McGarry was unable to get over the mountain and turned into a valley instead. Finally he rolled the plane over and fell out.

Rector watched the parachute blossom. As McGarry landed on the side of a hill he waved. Rector swooped down, lowered his flaps, then flung out a large candy bar. As he pulled up, he saw his friend walk away.

The loss of two of the best Tigers—McGarry and Newkirk—had a great psychological effect on the men at Loi-wing. Many began to grumble openly, not only about the dangerous strafing missions but about conditions in general.

All of the Flying Tigers were in poor physical shape and suffering from battle fatigue. Most of them were convinced they had been forgotten by their country and had been left to die far from home without the proper equipment. They had been beaten down by the deadly strain of more than five months of almost constant combat. Their contracts would soon expire and the majority were not anxious to push their luck in more combat. Many had become superstitious and dreaded their final missions. They wanted to stay alive.

Chennault sympathized with his men, but he had an additional problem. Now he was a brigadier general in the United States Army Air Forces and was being pressed by Stilwell to induct the AVG into the Army Air Forces. He opposed this vigorously and suggested that his pilots be given home leaves and then returned to fight in the same volunteer organization. He felt it was "criminal to sacrifice the spirit and experience of the group for a mere change in uniform."

But the Army argued that the paper work involved in keeping such an irregular organization supplied would be too great. Moreover, the Tigers couldn't be given furloughs for some time. Under protest Chennault agreed to try and persuade his men to enroll. But he made it clear that they would have to make their own decisions.

He sounded out the Tigers and found that almost every one was violently opposed to enlisting in the Army Air Forces. Chennault decided he should inform Chiang Kai-shek directly of this alarming state of affairs. On March 29 he radioed Madame Chiang, who handled all matters concerning the Flying Tigers. She spoke English fluently, and Chiang relied heavily on her judgment in affairs of state and strategy.

CAREFUL CHECK MAJORITY MEMBERS OF AVG REVEALS THAT NINETY (90) PERCENT WILL TERMINATE CON-

TRACTS RATHER THAN ACCEPT INDUCTION INTO U.S.
ARMY AIR FORCES IN CHINA. THIS ATTITUDE FIRM
DESPITE MY EARNEST PLEAS MAINTAIN GROUP REGARD-
LESS. MEN NOT UNPATRIOTIC BUT ALL HOPE GO HOME
BRIEF VISIT BEFORE FINAL ENTRY U.S. ARMY OR NAVY.

Two days later Harrison Forman of the New York
Times interviewed Chennault. The leader of the Flying
Tigers was outspoken and bitter. "Conversion [into the
United States Army Air Forces] would result in almost
complete loss of the effectiveness of my unit for a period
of a minimum of four months," he said.

"Moreover, breaking up of the AVG is not desired
either by the Chinese or the American people; and it
would be an event celebrated throughout Japan. My
Flying Tigers have made the Japs lose face—much
face—and the Nips don't like it."

But this story was censored by General Clayton Bissell, Stilwell's aviation officer, and neither the people
of the United States nor the Flying Tigers themselves
would know for years what the real situation was. Many
of the members of the AVG, not realizing that Chennault was fighting for them, began to resent him as well
as Vinegar Joe Stilwell.

3.

The new AVG advance base at Loi-wing was near the
model American village set up by William Pawley for
workers of the CAMCO factory. About twenty P-40s

95

were now being repaired at the plant. The Tigers lived in pleasant white cottages and spent their evenings at Pawley's luxurious country club. The Hell's Angels had painted a sign on the operations office—OLSON & CO., JAP EXTERMINATORS—24 HOUR SERVICE.

Fifteen days after Newkirk's death, Loi-wing was attacked for the first time. Approximately twenty-four Zeros approached the field several hours after dawn. Ten planes stayed at 8,000 feet while the rest dived on the field. But the Tigers had been warned. Eleven P-40s and four Hurricanes were already waiting at 17,000 feet.

As the attacking Zeros strafed the empty runways, Olson waggled his wings and led his flight through the clouds. In ten minutes the Tigers knocked down all but four of the strafers in a savage assault.

Then Tadpole Smith noticed the ten Zeros that were supposed to be protecting their bombers. Their pilots were circling above, completely unaware of the battle beneath the overcast. "If anyone isn't doing anything down there," Smith radioed, "come on up. Plenty of Zeros upstairs."

But the Japanese must have heard the message. They fled before the other Tigers could join Smith.

Two days later, five Zeros returned just after dawn. At the time of the attack there was a short radio blackout because of atmospheric conditions. Swooping in at treetop level the Japanese fighters shot up nine P-40s, then left. But when twenty-seven Japanese bombers arrived at 11:00 A.M. to complete the destruction, all the damaged Tomahawks had been repaired and were in the air. Because of the heavy overcast, there was no fight. The Japanese went home without doing any more damage.

Twenty Zeros came back at 3:00 P.M. Thinking the Tigers had been knocked out, they confidently dived on the field. But Tadpole Smith pounced on them with a flight of P-40s and Hurricanes which had been waiting in the clouds. The Tigers and R.A.F. pilots shot down eight Zeros. Not an Allied plane was lost.

4.

By mid-April, 1942, the resentment of the Flying Tigers—aggravated by the weeks of continual combat, lack of sleep and heavy losses—had reached a dangerous stage. To make matters worse, the Japanese were pushing farther and farther into Burma. Chiang Kai-shek kept asking Chennault for more and more strafing missions on the enemy's front-line positions. He also asked the Tigers to fly across the lines at low level. The Generalissimo explained that the mere sight of friendly aircraft encouraged the Chinese troops. These so-called morale missions irked the Tigers above all. Why should they risk their necks at low level just for show? Zeros were usually waiting above them, ready to pounce down.

Chennault strenuously objected to such missions and asked Chiang Kai-shek to cancel them. On April 20 he also protested to General Bissell in a radiogram:

A P-40 flying over the Burma Road provides air cover for Chinese
infantrymen in American helmets.

URGE IMMEDIATE APPEAL BY PRESIDENT ALL MEMBERS
AVG REMAIN ON DUTY HERE WITH PROMISE EARLY RE-
INFORCEMENT. GROUP LITERALLY WORN OUT NERVES
MORALE SHOT. PILOTS QUITTING BECAUSE OF PRESENT
EMPLOYMENT OF LOW ALTITUDE RECONNAISSANCE AND
LACK OF SUPPORT FROM ANY OTHER AIR UNIT. CAN
HOLD GROUP TOGETHER ONLY IF EMPLOYED PROPERLY
AS INTERCEPTOR PURSUIT. PLEASE CONSULT MADAME
CHIANG AND ADVISE AS IMMEDIATE DECISION NECESSARY.

The request that President Roosevelt write a personal appeal was sent on to Washington; but on the very next day, the Tigers were ordered to escort a group of R.A.F. Blenheim bombers on a mission to Chiengmai, Thailand.

Though Chennault was incensed, he plotted the mission and posted a list of the pilots who would go. But twenty-three of the pilots at Loi-wing, all worn with battle fatigue, protested strenuously. Tex Hill, who wasn't scheduled to go on the dangerous flight, tried to reason with these men and even offered to lead the mission. Ed Rector and three others promptly volunteered to go along.

The next day the twenty-three who had protested turned in their resignations. The matter was still undecided when a radiogram arrived from Madame Chiang. Received on April 23, three days after the trouble had started, it was an answer to Chennault's plea to discontinue strafing:

GENERALISSIMO CONSENTS USE OF AVG FOR FIGHTING JAP PLANES FIGHTING OUR TROOPS AND NOT FOR LOW ALTITUDE RECON.

Chennault was elated. The main cause of friction had been eliminated. He put the resignation list in a drawer.

On April 27 Chiang Kai-shek sent a message of praise to the AVG, along with an appeal to keep fighting.

"The entire Chinese nation has taken you to heart," he wrote, "and hails you as true comrades-in-arms. I feel certain that you will fight to a finish—to victory with the same ardent enthusiasm and tenacious will-to-win that have characterized your performances in the past."

The following day the AVG gave its answer—in battle. Fifteen Flying Tigers, led by Tex Hill and Olson, headed south looking for Japanese. After about an hour they spotted twenty-seven bombers heading for Loiwing. The Tigers swung around and saw a large group of Zero fighters weaving behind the bombers.

The Tigers attacked savagely and soon there were fights all over the sky. Twenty-two Zeros were shot down without a single loss. The Tigers had forgotten their brief revolt.

"Your President Is Greatly Concerned...."

1.

By the last week of April the Japanese had stormed up the Irrawaddy valley, crumpling the combined British and Chinese forces with ease. On April 29, one Japanese thrust reached Lashio, the last important Burmese city on the Burma Road. The escape route to China was now cut.

The Allied withdrawal was turning into a rout. Burmese natives, their long hatred of the British released, harassed the retreating columns. They sniped at stragglers and burned all foreign property.

Realizing the situation was hopeless, Stilwell ordered a DC-3 transport to pick him up at Shwebo, a city about sixty miles north of Mandalay. The next day Stilwell radioed Chennault at Loi-wing:

HAS MY PLANE ARRIVED YET FROM CHUNGKING EN ROUTE SHWEBO. CAN LOI-WING FIELD BE USED FOR FEW MORE DAYS. I WANT RETURN THERE SOON.

On May 1 Chennault replied:

CHINESE HAVE EVACUATED LOI-WING. AVG LEAVING TODAY.

That same morning at 11:00 A.M. Colonel Caleb Haynes arrived at Shwebo with the DC-3 from Chungking. Stilwell ordered some of his staff to fly to India to set up a temporary headquarters. But he refused to get aboard. Though almost sixty years old, he had decided to walk out with the rest of his men.

While Stilwell was leading his small party through the wild jungle toward India, complete disaster threatened China. Stilwell's Chinese army in northeast Burma was fleeing in disorder. Two regiments, however, did make a gallant stand near the Chinese border. They held off the enemy for three days, and then were outflanked.

The airfield at Loi-wing was now deserted. The wreckage of twenty-two damaged P-40s, burned at Chennault's order, was still smoking when the Japanese arrived on May 2. The following day a Tiger flew down the Burma Road and saw a Japanese column advancing into China.

"Vinegar Joe" Stilwell leads remnants of his battered forces through the wild Burmese jungles.

By May 5 the spearhead of the elite Japanese Red Dragon Armored Division approached the west bank of the Salween River. This was the last formidable barrier between the Japanese and Kunming. American Volunteer Group pilots reported that the armored column was moving toward the Salween through crowds of refugees. A disorganized mob of Chinese soldiers was fleeing just ahead of them. When Chennault heard this, he became greatly alarmed. There was nothing to stop the Japanese but the AVG.

If the enemy broke through to Kunming, China would be cut off from all foreign aid. She would have to surrender. Chennault felt there was only one solution—and that would mean the death of innocent refugees. He radioed Madame Chiang in Chungking:

LATEST REPORTS SAY JAPS ON WEST BANK SALWEEN RIVER 1500 HOURS 5 MAY. BRIDGE DESTROYED. JAPS MEETING NO OPPOSITION ANYWHERE AS SOLDIERS CIVILIANS PANIC STRICKEN FLEEING EAST ALONG ROAD. CONSIDER SITUATION DESPERATE AND JAPS MAY DRIVE TO KUNMING IN TRUCKS UNLESS ROADS AND BRIDGES DESTROYED AND DETERMINED OPPOSITION DEVELOPED. DUE TO FACT MANY CHINESE TRUCKS WEST OF SALWEEN PRESUMABLY IN HANDS OF ENEMY REQUEST AUTHORITY HIS EXCELLENCY THE GENERALISSIMO TO ATTACK TARGETS BETWEEN SALWEEN AND LUNGLING CITY.

Madame Chiang's answer soon arrived:

GENERALISSIMO INSTRUCTS YOU SEND ALL AVAILABLE AVG TO ATTACK TRUCKS BOATS ETC BETWEEN SALWEEN AND LUNGLING CITY. TELL AVG I APPRECIATE THEIR LOYALTY AND REDOUBLED EFFORTS PARTICULARLY AT THIS CRITICAL JUNCTURE.

Chennault quickly drew up his plan of attack. Recently a number of new model P-40s, Kittyhawks, had been ferried to Kunming. Unlike the Tomahawks, these had bomb racks. He decided to have four Kittyhawks bomb the armored column while four Tomahawks flew cover from above.

Chennault spoke to the men who had volunteered for the mission. If the Japanese were not stopped at the Salween River, he told them, China would have to surrender. Then he said somberly, "This is the most important point in the war."

A little after dawn the eight volunteers took off. Leading the flight of Kittyhawks was Tex Hill. With him was his old friend, Ed Rector, along with Frank Lawlor and Tom Jones. In addition to fragmentation bombs in the wing racks, each of their Kittyhawks carried a big demolition bomb in an improvised belly rack. Arvid Olson led the four Tomahawks that would be their cover. Upon these eight planes rested the fate of China.

Fifty miles from the Salween River, the Tigers saw huge bluish thunderheads to the south. Hill circled, studied the ominous clouds, and then flew directly into them. Soon the four fighter-bombers were being tossed by turbulent air. But in fifteen minutes they burst through into clear sky.

Just ahead Hill could see the muddy Salween winding down a deep gorge. Everything stood out with pinpoint clarity.

A Japanese engineering unit was hauling pontoons from trucks to the river's edge. Behind them, coiling like a great snake, was a long column of trucks and tanks. The Japanese Red Dragon Armored Division was trapped on the narrow road. To one side was a towering rock wall, to the other a steep precipice.

Hundreds of Allied trucks were abandoned during the Japanese advance along the Burma Road.

The four Kittyhawks dived; their target was the tail end of the column. To Hill and Rector it was like the old dive-bombing days on the *Yorktown*. One by one the four Tigers dropped their big demolition bombs. Their aim was good and the retreat of the Japanese was now partially blocked with landslides.

The Kittyhawks once more swooped down, spraying the trucks with fragmentation bombs. Ammunition and gasoline trucks exploded, tossing dozens of other vehicles into the gorge. Huge holes were ripped in the road.

Hill and his men turned and swept even lower. The

six .50-caliber machine guns of their Kittyhawks spewed lead into the column. When their ammunition was gone, Olson and his flight of Tomahawks dived down and strafed the trapped Japanese.

After the Tigers had returned safely to their base, the four Kittyhawks were reloaded with fragmentation and incendiary bombs. Hill, Rector and Lawlor were replaced but Jones argued so persuasively that Chennault let him return for the second raid.

The Japanese were still milling around in a daze when the AVG reappeared. The Tigers dropped more bombs, and the disciplined enemy troops began to run in terror. Dozens of fires raged along the winding road. Smoke rose in such clouds that the entire gorge looked as if it were on fire.

The Chinese soldiers trapped on the west side of the river now jumped out of their foxholes and began attacking the panic-stricken Japanese. Those on the other side of the Salween poured machine-gun fire into the fleeing column. But when the Tigers started back for home, all the Chinese stopped fighting long enough to stand up, wave their caps and cheer. For the first time in months, they had something to cheer about.

During the next four days Chennault attacked the Salween gorge and the Burma Road with every plane he had, even borrowing a flight of Curtiss Hawk-3 dive bombers and a dozen old Russian twin-engine bombers from the Chinese air force.

The Japanese stubbornly tried to force their way back toward the banks of the Salween but the AVG blasted every column that tried to move up. By May 11 the Japanese gave up trying. The drive into China was, momentarily, halted. The only military traffic moving on the Burma Road was heading south, in retreat.

2.

The AVG had held off the Japanese drive from Burma, but the Allied future in Asia was still black. China was cut off from the world except for the old Silk Route to Russia. Supplies and reinforcements could now come only by air from India over the rugged mountains. Vinegar Joe Stilwell was back in India after a rugged march of 140 miles through the wildest country. But he was a commander without an army, and with little prospect of getting one for some time.

China would still have to depend almost entirely on Chennault's Flying Tigers. And the Tigers were in bad shape. Half of their Tomahawks had been destroyed and others were under repair. The few flyable planes, including the newly arrived Kittyhawks, were kept in condition only by the constant labor and ingenuity of the ground crew.

Even more important was the steadily dwindling list of pilots. Seven instructors and a few Army Air Force men had been added to the roster but even these welcome replacements did little to solve Chennault's personnel problem.

On the day of the attack on Pearl Harbor, there had been eighty-five pilots. Of this original group, there

A mechanic overhauls the first P-40 to bring down a Japanese plane after the AVG became the 23rd Fighter Group.

were only fifty-two on May 17 and several of these were wounded and unable to fly. The ground crew had also been hard hit, particularly by thirty-seven resignations.

By now the personal appeal that Chennault had requested President Roosevelt to send to the AVG was posted on the headquarters bulletin board. It praised the AVG for "outstanding gallantry and conspicuous daring" and promised that "great numbers of new airplanes" would be sent to bring the 23rd Fighter Group (their new title) up to full strength. Other reinforcements were already on the way. It concluded:

> Leaves of absence should be given to A.V.G. veterans just as soon as replacements have absorbed your experience, training and tradition for rest and recuperation. It is planned that when replacements are adequately trained selected A.V.G. veterans will be recalled to the States or other theaters of operations to impart their combat experience and training to personnel in newly formed units.
>
> Your President is greatly concerned that the 23rd Group be fully supplied and kept in operation during the critical phase of the operations now pending. He has taken great pride in the worldwide acclaim given the Group and places great hope in its future fighting as rapidly as it is re-equipped.
>
> (signed) Franklin D. Roosevelt

The letter made little impression on the Flying Tigers. They still felt they had been badly treated, and they had no desire to be under the command of Stilwell's aviation officer, General Bissell.

The main objection of the Tigers was the Army's insistence that they continue on duty. They felt they had earned a thirty-day furlough so they could visit their families. By the end of May the situation was so bad that it was apparent only an about-face change in the attitude of Stilwell and Bissell would persuade the

Tigers to stay in China after July 4.

In the meantime, Chennault was faced with an even more immediate problem: the Japanese. The bombing season was about to begin and Chungking had to be defended. Chinese morale was so low, after the Burma defeat, that a few successful bombings of the capital might have serious consequences.

To bluff the Japanese away from Chungking, Chennault decided to make several surprise raids in east China. He left one squadron to defend Kunming and, on June 5, moved the others to Peishiyi, a field near Chungking. For several days Chennault's men flew back and forth over Chungking to make sure Japanese spies would know the Tigers were there in force.

The Americans lined the field at Peishiyi with rows of bamboo Tomahawk dummies. Then the two squadrons—with the exception of four planes which had orders to fly over Chungking at low altitude every day and pose as the entire force—were transferred to bases many miles to the east.

Now Chennault began to dive-bomb airfields and shipping at Hankow and Canton. The Japanese were so confused they stopped bombing cities and began concentrating on AVG airfields. The Tigers went up to meet every one of these attacks, and the score of victories rose. At last the battle was being fought on Chennault's terms.

The citizens of oft-bombed Kweilin were particularly grateful. On June 20 they feted the Tigers and issued this proclamation:

Guardians of the air, you heroes of the American Flying Tigers and the Chinese Divine Hawks:

After our long expectation and to our great cheerfulness you have annihilated eleven Japanese vultures in the air above Kweilin on June 13. This is the most brilliant merit of air combat that has ever been achieved at Kweilin. You have once more created your great glory of extinguishing your enemy in the air. We, the 300,000 citizens of Kweilin, are especially stimulated and delighted! While considering the cooperation between the U.S.A. and China for the common resistance against the aggressive violences, this is a particularly incomparable glory. We are sure that all the people of China and all the Allies will take this to be an everlasting token of remembrance.

Today we, the 300,000 citizens of Kweilin, are presenting you our heartiest congratulations and the highest respects to your comfort. And we are expecting your continual achievements of greater and richer merits with your inexhaustible heroism and bravery.

Let us yell:

"Long Live the American Flying Tigers.

"Long Live the Chinese Divine Hawks.

"Long Live cooperations between the U.S.A. and China."

(Signed) The Kweilin Airmen Comforting Evening Party

June 20, 1942

That same day the induction board, headed by Chennault, left Kunming in a DC-3 to begin visiting the various AVG bases. The first meeting was held at Kweilin on June 22, and the pilots politely listened to the board's pleas to join the AAF. Neale, who with 15½ victories was the leading ace, was offered a commission as lieutenant colonel. He turned it down. Other pilots were offered commissions as majors or captains. Not one accepted. Then the ground crew was assembled. These men also listened politely—and then refused to enlist.

The next morning Colonel Haynes, a member of the board, radioed Bissell:

FROM PRESENT OBSERVATIONS I DEEM IT IMPERATIVE THAT INDUCTION OF AVG BE DEFERRED UNTIL OCTOBER FIRST AND PRESENT CONTRACTS ETC BE CONTINUED. OTHERWISE OUR OPERATIONS ARE IN SERIOUS JEOPARDY. INDUCTION BOARD STRONGLY CONCURS IN ABOVE RECOMMENDATION.

At Hengyang, Tex Hill, who had just returned after ferrying a plane from India, was talking to Ed Rector.

"I saw the Old Man in Chungking," said Hill. "He told me everybody's going home, but someone with know-how has to stay and activate the new units. He wanted me to talk to you and some of the other fellows."

"I'm planning to go home," said Rector.

"So was I," said Hill. "But if all of us leave, this whole thing will fold up."

"I see he's sold you," said Rector. He grinned wryly. "I'll stay too."

Three other pilots—Charles Sawyer, Frank Schiel, Jr., and Gil Bright—followed their lead. So did five members of the staff and twenty-nine ground-crew men.

When Hill told Chennault of the decision to enlist, the General's leather face was impassive. It was as though he had always known Hill and Rector would stay with him. Then he asked Hill to talk to those pilots who had decided to go home. Would they volunteer to stay an extra two weeks until replacements arrived?

Johnny Petach, who had recently married the Tiger's red-haired nurse, Emma Foster, had already packed when Hill asked him to stay. Petach was anxious to take his bride back to the States but he agreed to fill in for two weeks. So did Neale, along with seventeen other pilots and a number of ground-crew men. As in every other emergency the Tigers had come through.

3.

On the night of July 3, 1942, the Chinese of Chungking presented Chennault with a gold sword in gratitude for the first bombless June since 1938. The next morning, the Fourth of July, the AVG at Kunming drove to the Peishiyi airfield for the last time. Jack Belden, the *Time-Life* correspondent who had known the Tigers since their first Rangoon battles, approached Tex Hill.

"People don't seem to understand you have feelings," said Hill, looking around at the dispersed P-40s. "When you work and fight together for a long time you hate to split up. It's like something going out of your life."

Belden then walked to Chennault's office for another interview.

"I have had the greatest opportunity an air officer of any nation ever had," said Chennault. "Not only was I able to satisfy my desire to prove my methods sound, but I was able to contribute to the common cause." Then he said sadly, "The AVG is the world's finest trained bunch of fighting airmen. Now I only look forward to meeting the enemy."

That afternoon Ed Rector and six of his men raided Hankow and on the way home knocked down five Japanese fighters. While they were gone, Bob Neale and three mates intercepted a dozen I-97s at Hengyang and shot down five. Then Neale and his wingman, Charlie Bond, saw two other Nakajimas, and gave chase. They knew it would be their last fight as Tigers.

Bond's target disappeared in clouds, but the weary Neale fought his opponent for twenty minutes. When Bond suddenly arrived and dived at the Japanese, Neale made a final pass and blew up the I-97.

The AVG had fought their last fight. Since their first wild action at Kunming on December 20, 1941, they had officially shot down 297 enemy planes. The actual score was probably nearer 600. In doing this they had killed at least 1,500 Japanese airmen and blown up equipment and supplies of incalculable value. More

General Chennault speaks at a dinner given in honor of the Flying Tigers. Madame Chiang Kai-shek and her husband are seated at his left.

important, they had kept open the key port of Rangoon, with the help of the R.A.F., for two and a half months. And at the Salween River they had stopped a Japanese drive which could have meant the end of China.

In addition, the American volunteers had saved east China cities from bombings that were sapping the hope of the people. On the back of Chennault's honorable discharge from the AVG, Madame Chiang wrote: "He performed the impossible."

All this was not done without sacrifice. Twenty-one Tigers had paid with their lives.

That evening the AVG of Peishiyi were entertained at the home of China's president, Lin Sen. Chennault was presented with an oil painting of Madame Chiang, the Generalissimo and himself. The Flying Tigers, whose off-duty exploits would be remembered in China as long as their deeds in the air, drank non-alcoholic punch and played musical chairs. Then Chiang Kaishek made a speech.

"General Chennault and his company of air knights," he said, "will always be remembered by the Chinese people as comrades-in-arms and as the friendly representatives of a friendly people."

At 11:00 P.M. the Tigers and their leader rode through the drizzle to their hostels. By the time they arrived it was midnight. The AVG had passed into history.

"Watch for the Fireworks!"

1.

Chennault was now under the command of General Bissell of the 10th U.S. Air Force, whose headquarters were in New Delhi, India. And what had been the AVG was now the China Air Task Force (CATF). It was composed of the 23rd Fighter Group and the 11th Bombardment Squadron. But the organization existed mostly on paper. Besides a handful of Mitchell bombers, Chennault had only 31 Tomahawks and 20 Kittyhawks.

The greatest shortage was in fighter pilots. In addition to Tex Hill, Ed Rector and the other three who had enlisted, there were eighteen Tigers staying on for an additional two weeks. There were also a dozen Army

Air Force pilots, only one of whom had seen combat.

The Japanese, assuming they were now facing only green pilots, immediately launched heavy attacks on Hengyang. But the new pilots, inspired by Hill and a few other veterans, knocked down thirty planes in two days. Four days later, on July 10, Johnny Petach, the recent bridegroom, led four ships on a raid against the town of Linchoun. Petach and Arnold Shamblin, another two-week volunteer, were shot down by ground fire. Shamblin was captured; Petach killed. Their loss particularly affected Hill, who had talked them into staying.

By July 19 all the volunteers had left except Bob Neale. On that day he came to Chennault to say good-bye, tears running down his cheeks. Only five of the original Tigers were left.

Rector, now a major, was put in command of Kweilin, the most strategic air base in east China. Hill, also a major, was given Hengyang. Both fields were little more than fighter strips with 3,000-foot runways built from crushed rocks and mud by hordes of Chinese workers.

Hill and Rector's squadrons worked under weather conditions that ranged from oppressive heat to sudden cold rains. The mechanics who struggled to keep the rickety planes aloft were attacked by insects as they worked far into the night in kerosene light. Most had no coveralls and worked in shorts to save their good uniforms. They had no spare parts and few tools.

The food was bad by American standards; dysentery and malaria became commonplace. The hostels were primitive, and the beds were constantly damp from the steaming heat. The China Air Task Force (CATF) was a unit of the United States Army Air Forces, but since it was cut off from the rest of the Allied world, the scrounging and improvisation continued. Dummy planes were made out of bamboo and straw. Belly fuel tanks, to give the planes more range, were constructed from bamboo and fish glue.

The Japanese soon recovered from the surprising resistance on July 5 and 6. They determined to wipe out the CATF and made plans to destroy Kweilin and Hengyang completely. To accomplish this they gathered a force of from 350 to 400 planes, including an elite fighter group provided with the new Japanese Zero— the Oscar. It was a great improvement over the original fixed-gear Zero, with more speed, fire power and ceiling.

The new offensive began on the evening of July 28 when five Japanese bombers took off. Their mission was simple: to put so many craters in the Hengyang runway that Hill's fighters couldn't take off the next morning.

Among Hill's new pilots were two men of exceptional ability and color. One was Captain Albert ("Ajax") Baumler, who had knocked down German and Italian planes as a Loyalist ace in the Spanish Civil War. The second was Major John R. Alison, Hill's deputy. He was short, lively and full of energy. Even the veteran Tigers admitted that Alison knew more about a P-40 than any other pilot. He had spent the past eight months in the U.S.S.R. teaching Russians how to fly the ship. Like

A Chinese ground crew prepares to outfit a P-40 with an extra "belly fuel tank" to give it a longer flying range.

Baumler he was eager to fight.

By midnight of July 28 Hill's men were all asleep in their hostel, a two-story gray barracks one mile north of the field. At 2:00 A.M. Alison heard Chinese boys running down the halls, shouting, "Jin-bao! Jin-bao!" ["Get up, please! Get up, please!"] It was an air raid!

The pilots ran outside and looked up at the black sky. They were not going to try and intercept. The P-40 was not a night fighter, and the last attempt at night-fighting in Rangoon had caused the death of a Tiger.

At last they could hear the hum of planes and then the *C-R-U-M-P* of bombs falling on their field. Alison saw the blue exhaust of the bombers and said, "If they come over again tomorrow night, I'm going up after 'em."

"I'll go with you," said Baumler.

Hill had been thinking about the same thing; in fact he and Chennault had already worked out a scheme. But he had another job to carry out first. At dawn he and four others took off from the gravel airstrip, avoiding the bomb craters not yet filled in by the Chinese. They headed toward Canton, but bad weather forced them to turn back. As Hill approached Hengyang, he heard the Chinese warning net report that an estimated seventy Japanese fighters were heading for the field. He knew that the Japanese usually listened in on the American combat radio frequency, so he began to call out orders to imaginary squadrons. His four men joined the game. By changing their voices, they gave the impression that they were at least forty strong. The seventy Japanese fighter planes promptly headed back home.

Soon after Hill returned to the base, he began preparations for the night interception. Chennault had told him, "At some point the Japanese bombers will cross your field. The only thing you won't know is their altitude."

Hill conferred with Baumler and Alison. Each man would orbit above the field at different altitudes, constantly circling to the left to avoid collision. "A man on the ground," said Hill, "will let you know when the

Four "Flying Tigers": (left to right) John Alison, Tex Hill, Albert Baumler, and Mack Mitchel.

Japs cross the field. Then attack."

Baumler and Alison parked their Kittyhawks at the north end of the strip, parachutes in the cockpits. Everything was ready for a quick take-off. A little after 2:00 A.M. the next morning, Alison was wakened by a clanking sound. A Chinese boy was hurrying down the porch hallway banging on a tin can and shouting, "Jinbao, please!"

Alison and Baumler dressed quickly and ran to a waiting Ford station wagon. The Ford raced to the north end of the runway. The two pilots climbed onto the wings of their planes, lowered themselves into their cockpits. Their engines coughed and then roared. Alison taxied down the darkened strip. At ninety miles an hour the ship began to bounce, and he pulled back on the stick. As Alison's plane climbed, Baumler began his take-off. They circled to the left to their assigned altitudes. Baumler went to 8,000 feet, Alison to 12,000.

Tex Hill, dressed only in a Burmese loincloth, stayed on the ground to direct the attack. Finally he heard the drone of Japanese bombers. Then he saw dim shapes approaching. "They're coming in," he called into the microphone. "They're making a run from north to south." He waited for his pilots to answer. There was only dead silence.

When Alison heard Hill he scanned the sky above. Nothing was in sight. The ground radio told him that the Japanese had passed over the field but were making a turn and heading back north. This time he looked up and saw six bluish flames—the exhausts of three twin-engined bombers flying in V formation.

"I've got 'em in sight!" he yelled into his microphone.

John R. Alison

"They're above me. Watch for the fireworks!"

He began a right climbing turn and soon was behind the bombers. When almost within range, the three Japanese turned to the right. Alison, taken by surprise, banked right. Now he was very close, and between the glaring moon and the Japanese. They saw him and began to fire. From point-blank range, shells smashed into the Kittyhawk's engine and the instrument board.

Down below, Hill saw the blast of Alison's six machine guns. When nothing happened he said to himself, "He's missed them."

Instead of diving to safety, Alison bored in closer and fired at one Japanese plane. Shells from another bomber slammed into Alison's P-40 but he doggedly hung on, hoping he could blow up his target before his own ship flamed up. A chunk of burning phosphorus burned into his left arm. He knocked it away and fired again.

The bomber in his sights swung wildly up and to the left, badly wounded. Suddenly Baumler appeared, tagging behind the faltering Japanese ship. He fired and there was a burst of flames. Now he could claim victories over the entire Axis—German, Italian and Japanese.

By this time Alison had turned right and was going after the bomber that had been hitting him. Though his P-40 was spewing out black smoke, Alison swung in behind the Japanese and fired his six guns. He saw sparks on the bomber's wing near the gas tank and knew his aim was good. He fired again. All at once there was a brilliant orange explosion.

Down below, Hill and the others saw the two bursts of flame. The sky was alight. It was an awesome sight.

Alison was already on the tail of the third bomber, which was just dropping its load on the runway. He fired at the wing tanks for he had only a few hundred rounds left. Chunks of the bomber flew off and flames erupted. The bomber started down as its crew piled out, their parachutes aflame.

But Alison's motor was coughing. He yanked back on the throttle but it was no use. He could have bailed out but he wanted to land the badly needed ship. As he started down, he saw another flaming torch in the sky. Baumler had caught a fourth bomber.

Hill heard a motor cut out and knew it was Alison's. Then he saw Alison's ship approaching the field. The P-40 slipped off, but overshot the field. It straightened out and there was a brief roar as Alison tried to gun the motor. Then the engine burst into flames. Hill was sure Alison could not survive.

At that moment another alert sounded. A wave of bombers was coming in from Hankow. Hill, still wearing only a loincloth, ran to his plane, jumped in. A jeep at the end of the field threw the beams of its lights down the runway. Baumler was landing. As he taxied to the side, Hill gained speed. Bombs began to fall before his wheels left the ground.

He climbed so he could see the bombers. He would follow them home and pick them off as they landed. He got to 10,000 feet but the Japanese were still not in sight. He started north hoping to find them.

Before reaching Hankow he was sure he saw a bomber down below. He turned on his gun switch and dived 5,000 feet. Suddenly he had a feeling of apprehension and realized he was aiming at the ground. He pulled up sharply and saw there were mountains on both sides.

He continued to Hankow but, when he saw nothing, turned back. As he neared Hengyang, he radioed for lights. Soon he saw six tiny gleams and knew the ground crew had placed tung oil lanterns on each side of the runway. He lowered his wheels. Just then a stick of yellow phosphorus bombs blossomed across the runway. Phosphorescent craters glared at him like big cats' eyes. He pulled up, almost spinning in. He leaned his gas mixture since he was almost out of fuel and stayed aloft until the sun rose. Then he landed between the gaping bomb craters. Back at the base he learned that nothing more had been heard from Alison.

Several hours later there was another alert. Hill took off with nine other pilots. Soon thirty-five Oscars, the improved Zeros, swept in from the north in a loose V formation.

Those below saw a show as astounding as the one the night before. From the opposite direction, the ten P-40s were charging directly at the mass of Oscars.

Hill was aiming at the Japanese leader. The two rushed head on, all guns blazing, like gun fighters of the Old West. Those watching were sure the two ships would ram. At the last second, the Oscar pulled up in one direction while Hill pulled up in another. As the ships passed, Hill was positive they would crash. Instinctively he ducked his head. The Oscar was smoking, but it circled the field, then dived deliberately into a row of dummy P-40s.

Alison, as it turned out, had been watching the duel from afar. He had ditched into the Siang River, saving his ship as well as his life. Shortly afterward Alison received the Distinguished Service Cross; Baumler, the Distinguished Flying Cross.

In spite of the mounting losses, the Japanese kept hammering at Hengyang, determined to blast Hill's squadron out of existence. The night and day bombings continued until the pilots and ground crew were almost worn out from exhaustion.

One evening Hill flew solo to Hankow and dive-bombed the Japanese pilots preparing to take off. He kept them so occupied there was no raid on Hengyang that night and his weary men finally got an undisturbed sleep. For this he was given a Silver Star.

For the next three days the Japanese made a final all-out attempt to wipe out Hengyang, losing twenty-one planes while Hill lost only two. Then, on August 5, more than forty Oscars attacked Hengyang. Alison led the counterattack. Lee Minor was hit from the rear unexpectedly and became the first regular Army Air Force pilot in China to give his life. Although it was a bad day for the Americans, the Japanese began to realize that the CATF would be as hard to eliminate as the Flying Tigers. The costly assaults on Hengyang stopped.

Target for Today: Hong Kong

1.

By the beginning of September, 1942, Chennault's hard-fighting CATF had dwindled to thirty-eight pilots and thirty-four flyable P-40s. They had only enough gas for two days. Then supplies began coming by air across "the Hump"—the rugged mountains between Kunming and India. With the Burma Road closed this was now the only supply route to China. During the next two years an incredible amount of war material was flown into China at great risk to pilots and crews.

In addition to the sorely needed supplies coming over the Hump, the reinforcements Chennault had been promised in June finally arrived. These consisted of six more B-25 Mitchell bombers, some worn-out P-40s and twenty well-trained Army Air Force pilots who had been defending the Panama Canal.

Late in September the monsoon season ended and the weather was again good for fighting in the air and on the ground. Chennault's spies in occupied territory confirmed air reconnaissance reports that the Japanese would soon drive up the Burma Road and once more try to cross the Salween River.

Chennault countered by attacking convoys on the Burma Road in regular fighter sweeps. He sent his Mitchells as far south as Lashio, bombing key bridges, dumps and airfields.

His biggest worry was how to deal with the new Japanese Zero fighters: the Oscars, twin-engined Nicks and clipped-wing Hamps. All these models could easily climb to 25,000 feet. Even at this altitude they performed well whereas the P-40 began faltering at 20,000 feet. Since Chennault always insisted on fighting where his men had the advantage, he devised a plan to lure the Japanese fighters down to the altitude where the P-40 fought its best. Like all his tactics, this plan was simple. He would send his bombers on a mission at an altitude of 15,000 feet. The P-40s, meanwhile, would be hovering out of sight several thousand feet above. When the Japanese struck at the bomber bait, the P-40s would pounce on them.

To make this trap work, Chennault needed an extremely important target—one that the Japanese would have to defend. After much thought he picked Hong

Kong, a major staging area for Japanese convoys surging into the southwest Pacific. For a week Chennault and his chief of staff, Colonel Merian C. Cooper, worked almost around the clock, plotting the raid. Cooper, the director of "King Kong" and other famous movies, had flown as a combat pilot in the First World War. He had been assigned to go to Russia on a special mission but after waiting in vain for his visa in Chungking he became impatient and flew to Kunming. He told Chennault he "wanted a job with an outfit that was fighting."

On October 15 Chennault and Colonel Cooper held a meeting in Kunming with Stilwell and Bissell. The

Left to right: General Henry Arnold, General Claire Chennault, General Joseph Stilwell, Sir John Dill and General Clayton Bissell tour a Flying Tiger base in China.

plans for the Hong Kong raid were approved, but the weather suddenly broke and thick clouds covered most of China for nine days. Finally on October 24 Chennault's warning net in east China reported that the skies were clearing.

Chennault ordered his bombers loaded, fueled and checked. Late that afternoon he and Cooper flew east to the jumping-off point, Kweilin, which was less than 350 miles from Hong Kong. While Chennault was establishing his headquarters in the cave that was Ed Rector's operations office, Cooper and a few other officers went into town. There they spread rumors about a big raid they were going to make the next morning on Canton. Cooper well knew that at least one Japanese spy would hear them, and all available enemy fighter planes would be gathered in the Canton area—some eighty air miles northwest of Hong Kong.

At eight the next morning the planes from Kunming began to arrive at Kweilin, a few at a time. Twelve bombers and twelve fighters had left Kunming, but five P-40s developed engine trouble and turned back. Thus only seven fighters would fly protective cover.

The pilots rushed to Chennault's cave and were hurriedly briefed. Kweilin was only a short flight from several Japanese air bases, and an unexpected raid could wipe out the entire striking force. After Chennault outlined his plan, Caleb Haynes pointed out the targets on a large wall map. Haynes was to lead the bombers.

"If you see any battleships here," he said, "attack

them. Otherwise everybody should concentrate on the docks, warehouses and installations here." His finger ran down Hong Kong's water front. Haynes, who had recently been promoted to brigadier general, was extremely eager to hit Hong Kong, for strictly personal reasons. The Japanese radio had recently said there was nothing to fear from United States bombers in China since they were commanded by "an old broken-down transport pilot named Haynes."

2.

At 11:45 A.M. the seven P-40s roared down the Kweilin runway. Their leader was Colonel Robert Scott who had taken over command of the 23rd Fighter Group when Bob Neale went home. Scott had always wanted to be a fighter pilot but was told he was too old. After the attack on Pearl Harbor, he volunteered to fly supplies over the Hump to China and made several trips in this capacity. Then he talked Chennault into letting him fly a P-40—as protection for other transport planes.

In addition to flying these missions, Scott on his own began strafing the Japanese on the Burma Road. But even this wasn't action enough for him. With Chennault's tacit permission he became an unofficial member of the AVG and on occasion flew combat missions as a wingman with the Flying Tigers. In spite of all his combat time, Scott had yet to destroy an enemy plane. As he left the Kweilin runway, he was eager for his first victory.

Through the clouds of red dust churned up by the P-40s, the twelve bombers lumbered down the field. They circled the field and headed east in four flights of three planes each. There was a sharp rattle as the gunners tested their weapons. Hovering over the bombers at 20,000 feet were Scott and his fighter cover.

Halfway to the target, the whole formation swung south so they would pass thirty miles below Canton and not alert its fighter fields. Soon they swept over the lowlands cut up by canals and numerous rice paddies. Then came the sharp smell of salt water, and the airmen saw the South China Sea.

Scott split his fighters in two groups. He kept Tex Hill and two others with him. The remaining three swung to the left of the bombers. The entire formation turned and headed up the coast. It flew over Portuguese Macao, a famed spy rendezvous for both sides. In less than fifteen minutes the planes neared a rocky, mountainous island only half again larger than Manhattan. This was Hong Kong, a few minutes' ride by ferry to China. In peacetime the narrow bay between the island and the mainland city of Kowloon was filled with thousands of junks, ketches, and sampans. Now approximately ten freighters were lying at anchor there.

General Haynes led the bombers over Hong Kong to a point seven miles north of Kowloon, then turned south in preparation for the bomb run. Suddenly twenty-six Zero fighters appeared and swept through the last three B-25s. Shells began plowing into Captain Allers' bomber. One engine coughed and stopped.

Robert L. Scott

Lieutenant Morton Sher shoved the stick of his P-40 down and dived to the rescue. He blasted one Zero to bits. While he was shooting down a second, other Japanese fighters put his plane out of commission. Sher leaped out. As he parachuted to earth, two P-40s kept guard so he wouldn't be strafed.

Tex Hill heard Allers' radioman shout, "Can't stay up with formation. Attacked by Zeros!" Hill looked around but couldn't find the stricken B-25. Just then he heard Scott calling excitedly, "Bandits ahead . . . Zeros! At eleven o'clock!"

Hill said, "Yes, I see 'em," and plunged into battle. Scott was also diving at a Zero. He checked a bit

135

nervously several times to make sure his gun switch was on before dropping his fifty-gallon bamboo belly tank. Then he rolled the P-40 on its back to get more speed. When he was not much more than 1,000 yards from his target, Scott began firing.

He missed but kept boring in. Suddenly Tex Hill cut in front of him, his six machine guns spitting. The Zero flamed as Hill spun from his tight turn. Scott got behind another Zero and fired. He zoomed by so close he could see the pilot's head inside the glass canopy. Smoke was pouring back. He had his first victory.

By this time Allers' B-25 had plunged 11,000 feet. As he finally was about to bring up his ship, half a dozen Japanese fighters swarmed toward him. His top gunner saw a Zero turning at their level and fired. First the Zero's tail section came off in pieces, and then the rest of the ship flew apart. Immediately another Zero made a pass. The top gunner and Lieutenant Joe Cunningham both fired. The Japanese plane exploded, tumbling into the ocean.

Now Allers' one good engine was on fire. Finally it sputtered and went dead. Allers headed for China, ordering his crew to bail out. Two jumped. Lieutenant Nicholas Marich, the co-pilot, and Cunningham were ready, but the bombardier was still struggling to get into his chute. His straps were too short. They were now down to 2,000 feet.

Allers lined the bomber up on a rice paddy and Marich shouted, "It's too late to hit the silk! We're going to crash-land!"

The B-25 plowed into the paddy but didn't tip over. Allers fired seven bullets into the Norden bomb sight but, as the crew prepared to burn the plane, three Zeros swept down to strafe. The men ran for cover; one shell hit Allers' foot.

The other eleven American bombers were moving over their target in spite of black puffs of flak. The bomb-bay doors of Haynes' ship were open. The yellow lights on the bomb panel indicated that the bombs were ready. Lieutenant Colonel Herbert ("Butch") Morgan, the bombardier, pulled the switch and called into the interphone, "They're off!"

The lights on the bomb panel went off. Far below, the yellow bombs were tumbling toward the center of the Kowloon docks. Now bundles of rice-paper pamphlets were pushed through the bomb bay. These had been printed at General Haynes' own expense and read, in both English and Japanese: "These bombs come with the compliments of the old broken-down transport pilot Haynes."

Flak increased and four bursts hit Haynes' bomber, but no one was hurt. Down below, dozens of huge puffs billowed up from the docks so rapidly that the white smoke was quickly transformed into enormous black clouds. Only a few bombs missed. Soon fire and smoke covered the entire Kowloon water front.

As Zeros swarmed at the bombers, General Haynes abruptly shoved the nose of his ship down. The other bombers did the same. The surprised Japanese now found themselves under the concentrated fire of all the

Mitchells. They couldn't pass through this formidable formation which was diving slightly, full throttle, wing inside wing.

Two Japanese fighters headed for Haynes' ship. The turret gunner hit one enemy plane, and it blew up. Then he swung his gun at the second Zero, which was above and behind. After one burst the Zero slid off and, as it went plunging down, exploded.

The P-40s were also picking off the interceptors rapidly. To Tex Hill the falling Japanese planes looked like little candles. Near by Scott was tangling with four twin-engine planes, Messerschmitt 109s. He winged one Messerschmitt and, as it smoked and fell in a long, wide loop, he tagged behind, pumping lead into its tail. He doggedly kept firing until the enemy caught on fire and plunged into the water.

Scott was the last to return to Kweilin. As he came over the field he performed a victory roll, then landed. "General," he excitedly told Chennault, "I got four definitely!"

Chennault's fliers claimed a total of eighteen planes shot down, but this was too modest an estimate. That night a Japanese radio announcer said, "Only twenty of our fighters were lost in repulsing the American bombers." The cost to the Americans had been one bomber and one P-40. (Lieutenant Sher, the fighter pilot, reported back a week later. The following week Marich, Cunningham and another crew member walked into Kweilin. Allers and the other two crew members

Following their safe return to the Kweilin base, Lieutenants Nicholas Marick and Joseph Cunningham tell of their experiences inside Japanese lines after having been shot down during the October 25 raid on Hong Kong. Left to right: Cunningham, Merian Cooper, Butch Morgan (holding a Japanese fragmentation bomb), Marick and Ed Rector.

were captured.)

As soon as the bombers landed, the pilots were fed and briefed for a second mission. Half would go after the Hong Kong power plant, and the rest would attack the main fighter airdrome at Canton.

Just after midnight Chennault was sitting in the cave

at Kweilin listening to the warning-net reports of the second mission. In approximately twelve hours he planned to strike the docks and ships around Hong Kong again. He would keep at it until all the gas and bombs were gone.

Then an urgent radio message came from Bissell's 10th Air Force headquarters in Delhi:

BOMB LASHIO AND MYITKYINA AIRDROMES UNTIL FURTHER NOTICE BEGINNING AT DAWN.

Chennault was furious. Just as he had Hong Kong reeling, he was ordered to turn in the other direction and hit Burma. Why couldn't the 10th Air Force, which was much closer, do the job? In spite of his feelings, he sent the bombers to Burma as soon as they returned from Canton and Hong Kong.

But he still wanted another strike at Hong Kong. He loaded every available P-40 with a 500-pound bomb and sent this force to dive-bomb ships in Victoria Harbor. At least one tanker and several freighters were sunk, but Captain P. B. O'Connell was lost in a daring attack on the tanker.

Though some workers had been killed in the raids, the morale of the Chinese in Hong Kong soared. At last there was hope. The Japanese yen began to drop in value, and soon it was against the law even to discuss the raids.

When Chennault learned of the great psychological

General Chennault chats with a pilot while his pet dachshund Joe stands on the wing of the fighter plane.

effect of these raids, he was determined to launch another series. In November he returned to Kweilin to make arrangements.

He walked into Rector's cave, followed as usual by his ever-present companion, a dachshund named Joe. Rector had once asked Chennault why the dog was so faithful. Chennault said he had trained Joe to be a retriever. One day, while Chennault was hunting near Kunming, Joe leaped into a lake to bring back a bird his master had only winged. The big goose kept beating Joe over the head with its one good wing. When Chennault saw the persistent Joe was drowning, he took off his boots, jumped into the lake and saved him.

"Up to that day," said Chennault, "that dog liked me. Afterwards he *loved* me."

While Chennault was finishing his conference in the Kweilin cave, Joe spotted a rat deep in the cave and scuttled after it. Chennault kept shouting, "Come here, hound," but the dog refused to return. Although his plane was waiting to take him back to Kunming, Chennault sat down, saying, "Well, he'll have to come out sometime."

Two hours later Joe emerged, filthy and panting. The annoyed Chennault grabbed the dog. Then without saying a word to Rector, he walked to the plane and tossed Joe aboard.

The new raids began on November 23 with a strike on shipping in the Gulf of Tonkin. The next day, Chennault's bombers moved north and surprised the Japanese at the main Canton air base. Only two fighters got off the ground, and these were knocked down. Some forty-two planes were destroyed on the runway.

Chennault kept varying his targets, throwing the Japanese into such confusion they had no idea where he would strike next.

On the morning of November 27 he assembled his

biggest force: fourteen bombers and twenty-two P-40s. The target was Canton, where the Japanese had a large group of fighters. Just before noon the big American striking force took off, flew low over Kweilin and headed north. Once out of sight of possible local spies, the raiders turned toward Hong Kong. The fighters climbed to 20,000 feet, several thousand feet above the bombers.

In an hour they could see the hills of Hong Kong island and beyond it the usual fog banks of the South China Sea. Suddenly the formation swung sharply to the south—and Canton. Once more Chennault had tricked the Japanese, who were waiting in Hong Kong. The bombers flew over the great Whampoa docks at Canton and dumped their loads.

Within minutes two freighters were burning. As the formation began wheeling back to the north, the leader of the bombers, Butch Morgan, called, "California!" and started for Kweilin.

Only then did the Japanese fighters rise from their Canton bases to do battle. But Chennault's P-40s had the advantage of altitude and dived at the enemy like hawks. Fights ranged all over the sky, but the conflict was one-sided. Zeros were plummeting down like stricken birds. Scott ordered one man to escort the bombers to Kweilin. The rest of the Americans continued picking off the dazed Japanese fighters. The new pilots—Johnny Alison, Bruce Holloway and others— were proving worthy successors to the original Flying Tigers.

Thanks largely to Chennault's deception, twenty-seven

143

Standing, left to right: Clinton Vincent, John Alison, Bruce Holloway.
Kneeling: Albert Baumler and Grant Mahoney.

Japanese were knocked down. It was one of the greatest air victories in Asia, greatly appreciated by the millions of Chinese spectators in Canton.

The next day the CATF ended its second series of raids with a strike at shipping in the Gulf of Tonkin. In six days Chennault's men had pounded targets eight hundred miles apart. They had destroyed seventy-one planes, three ships and innumerable supplies, at a cost of only gasoline and bombs. Not a plane, not a man had been lost.

3.

For several months Tex Hill and Ed Rector had been sick with dysentery and malaria. And for some time Chennault had been requesting that they be sent home on leave; but General Bissell turned down the requests. After one dive-bombing attack on a gunboat—for which he eventually got a Distinguished Flying Cross—Hill was so sick he could barely climb out of his cockpit.

At last, late in November, permission came from

Left: Chennault pins a Distinguished Flying Cross on the tunic of Major Edward F. Rector. Right: He bids good-by to two of his aces—Rector and Hill—before they return to the States for well-earned leaves.

Delhi for the two Flying Tigers to return to the United States for their well-earned leaves. Hill called his squadron together to give a short farewell speech. "If possible," he concluded, "I should like to return to the seventy-fifth after my leave." Then he turned the squadron over to Major Alison and started for India.

Rector was already on his way to an Indian hospital. But both would return to Chennault.

4.

The argument about Hill and Rector was only one of the bitter clashes between Chennault and Bissell. Chennault was annoyed by having to deal with the Chinese first through Bissell's headquarters in India and then Stilwell's headquarters in Chungking. It was, he wrote Stilwell, "unwieldy, illogical and unnecessary."

Late in January, 1943, Stilwell cut in half the deliveries of gas to the CATF. This meant there would be only 350 gallons a day, scarcely enough to warm up the engines and taxi to the runways. Consequently Chennault flew to Stilwell's headquarters to protest.

When Chennault insisted that the CATF would have to be grounded, the order was not put into effect. But even 700 gallons was not enough. Chennault was soon forced to ground his planes for twenty-two days.

Not long after Chennault returned from his meeting with Stilwell, Colonel Scott was ordered to fly to Washington, D.C., at once "for duty in the Office of the Chief of Army Air Forces." Chennault walked with Scott to the transport that was taking his fighter commander back to America.

"Tell them the truth about China," he said to Scott. "Get the facts to the people and get me some planes out here. I can win this war . . . But you've got to talk."

In Washington Scott was brought to the War Room of the Army Air Forces. Here he told senior officers of all the services of the air battles in China won by Americans in obsolete P-40s at a ratio of fourteen to one.

When he had finished, General Arnold said, "Scott, you just told us the P-40 was obsolete. How then do you explain its record out there against new Jap Zeros?"

"Chennault," said Scott. "General Chennault made the difference, sir."

"I'm Glad That Man Is on Our Side...."

1.

Chennault was promoted to major general on March 3. A week later the CATF became the 14th U.S. Air Force. On paper this was a formidable organization, but in actuality little had changed. Chennault's greatest fight was not against the Japanese but for enough supplies to keep his planes in the air.

By now the trouble between Chennault and Vinegar Joe Stilwell had reached the boiling point. Stilwell, a staunch advocate of ground warfare, thought Chennault's idea of fighting the major war in China's skies was ridiculous. Planes, he felt, should merely help the infantry win the battle on the ground—where, in his

148

opinion, all battles were won. Air power would never stop a strong ground attack. And he doubted the ability of the Chinese to defend Chennault's advanced airfields.

The relationship between Stilwell and Chiang Kai-shek was far worse. The Generalissimo had no confidence in Vinegar Joe's abilities and felt China was doomed as long as Stilwell remained in command. Stilwell, in turn, did not even try to hide his own bitterness.

At this time Wendell Willkie, who had been defeated by Roosevelt in the 1940 presidential election, arrived in China. The President had sent him on a round-the-world trip as his personal envoy. Willkie was shocked by the state of affairs he found in China. He asked Chennault to write him a detailed letter so the President would know the difficulties of the 14th Air Force.

Others added their pleas for more aid to Chennault. Dr. T. V. Soong wrote Roosevelt's special adviser, Harry Hopkins, that Chennault should be called to Washington to discuss the matter at the conference Roosevelt and his military leaders would soon hold with the British.

Several weeks later, on April 10, Chiang Kai-shek himself radioed Roosevelt:

I WOULD URGE THAT YOU SUMMON GENERAL CHEN-
NAULT TO WASHINGTON TO LAY BEFORE YOU AND GEN-
ERAL ARNOLD THE PLAN I HAVE BEEN DISCUSSING WITH
HIM. I BELIEVE THIS IS MOST NECESSARY IN ORDER TO
MAKE EFFECTIVE OUR MUTUAL DESIRE TO STRIKE THE
ENEMY BY AIR. . . .

Stilwell's supporters in Washington were just as busy. General George C. Marshall, the Chief of Staff, did not feel that Chennault alone should be called to the capital. He suggested that Stilwell and Bissell accompany Chennault. Roosevelt agreed that Stilwell should come but crossed Bissell's name off the list.

Marshall immediately radioed the news to Stilwell. On April 20 Vinegar Joe flew to Kunming. When Chennault met him at the plane Stilwell asked in surprise, "Where are your bags? Aren't you ready to go?"

"Go where?" Chennault had no idea what he was talking about.

Stilwell took Chennault behind the plane and in an undertone explained about the Washington conference. It was only on the long plane ride to the United States that Chennault began setting down a written plan for future air strategy. He knew he must convince Roosevelt and Churchill that advanced bases behind enemy lines, as well as increased supplies, men and planes, were necessary to win the war in China. He used a brief case, held on his lap, as a desk and wrote with a pen that leaked at high altitudes. But by the time the big plane landed at Washington, the draft was completed.

The first meeting of the important Anglo-American conference—it was called "Trident"—was held at the White House at 2:30 P.M., May 12. Chennault still did not have a regulation uniform. He wore a prewar olive-drab blouse, a gray wool shirt and black tie. Some of the British wondered what nation he represented. When

The General props his briefcase on his knees and prepares to work during a flight.

Churchill saw the stern man with the leathery, lined face, he is reported to have said, "I'm glad that man is on our side."

Chennault, eager to defend his plan face-to-face with

his critics, was brief but graphic. He suggested using China as a platform to mount a great air offensive against Japan. All he asked was a force of 150 fighters, 70 medium bombers, 35 heavy bombers—and enough supplies and gas to operate them. This offensive, he said, should start in July when good fighting weather broke over east China.

Stilwell objected strenuously. Increased air activity would only provoke the enemy into an offensive and the east China air bases would be captured. He suggested, instead, a ground campaign to recapture Burma.

General Marshall and Secretary of War Henry Stimson backed Stilwell. But Roosevelt was swayed by Chennault's plan to bomb ships in the Formosa Straits and the South China Sea. He asked Chennault if the new air force in China could sink a million tons of shipping a year.

"If we receive 10,000 tons of supplies monthly," was Chennault's quick answer, "my planes will sink and severely damage *more* than a million tons."

Roosevelt banged his fist on the desk. "If you can sink a million tons, we'll break their back."

Churchill agreed and Chennault's plan was approved. When the conference concluded, Churchill asked Chennault to pay him a visit in Great Britain. But Chennault refused. Kunming had just been badly bombed twice, and he was anxious to get back to China.

The morning Chennault was to leave he was called to the White House. Roosevelt asked if he had gotten everything he wanted at the conference. Yes, said Chennault, and if he got the supplies, he would keep his promise to sink a million tons a year.

After Chennault had explained the tactical plans for the offensive, the President leaned back in his chair. "Now I want you to write me from time to time," he said, "and let me know how things are getting along."

"Do you mean you want me to write to you personally?"

"Yes, I do."

2.

More planes started coming into Kunming. Big B-24 Liberators began landing with crews ready for action. Chennault's guerrilla air force was rapidly turning into a powerful striking force.

But the supplies promised at Trident failed to arrive on schedule, and Chennault was forced to cut down his operations. By the end of summer supplies still lagged. Chennault sent his chief of staff, Clinton ("Casey") Vincent, to Washington with a personal letter to Roosevelt:

We have not been given the tools to do the job. . . .

We have succeeded in defeating the Japanese repeatedly only because of the courage, aggressiveness, and determination of our air and ground crews. At this time in the war, American combat units should not be forced to fight against such superior odds as the Japanese possess in China. . . .

Casey Vincent and Chennault

At this time Chennault also asked that Tex Hill be sent back to China. Hill was now teaching pilots at Eglin Field, Florida, telling them what he had learned as a Flying Tiger. When he heard that the "Old Man" wanted him, Hill discussed the proposed transfer with his recent bride. Chennault needed him in China because of his experience. He felt he should go. His wife agreed.

Hill was given two jobs. He was made deputy to Vincent and commander of the fighter group. Together Vincent and Hill planned the first bombing of the island of Formosa. Their target was Shinchiku, a large bomber base and combat-training center.

The operation was so secret that only Vincent and Hill knew what the destination would be when the bomber and fighter pilots gathered for the final briefing.

On Thanksgiving Day, 1943, twelve B-25s took off from a base two hundred and fifty miles east of Kweilin. It was so close to Formosa that long-range fighters— P-38s and P-51As—could escort the bombers. Hill led the fighters toward the Formosa Straits. Upon reaching the sea, he descended and headed for Formosa, just skimming the waves.

The low-flying planes caught the Japanese completely by surprise. As Hill's planes swept over Shinchiku, a

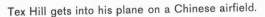

Tex Hill gets into his plane on a Chinese airfield.

long string of Japanese bombers were just approaching the field with wheels down. In a minute they all were smoking wrecks. Only seven or so fighters got off the field, and these were knocked down rapidly.

The American fighters strafed rows of parked planes, then climbed to cover the Mitchell bombers which were coming in. The B-25s scattered their fragmentation bombs and strafed planes and fleeing men. At least forty Japanese bombers were destroyed.

Soon Chennault's advanced air bases were proving their worth. Two of Japan's most vital waterways—the Yangtze and the South China Sea—were under constant attack. Raw materials flowing back to Japan from the conquered territories were being choked off. In the first month of 1944, some 56,900 tons of shipping were sunk. In February this was raised to 65,000 tons.

Chennault was so enthused by these sucesses that he wrote another personal letter to President Roosevelt guaranteeing to sink even more than he had promised— if the promised supplies were sent.

Roosevelt replied:

I agree with the importance of the plan against shipping as part of the effective flank attack on Japan from China. Your figures on results of operations against Japanese shipping are excellent. You are the doctor and I approve your treatment.

But the supplies to Chennault still lagged far behind promises. In March his spies warned that the Japanese

Billowing clouds of smoke rise from the Hengyang Airfield base as General Chennault prepares to abandon it to the advancing Japanese.

were mounting a powerful assault on east China. Chennault promptly warned Roosevelt, Stilwell and Arnold that China was in mortal danger. He could not counter the attacks unless more tonnage were quickly delivered. He wrote Roosevelt:

> I wish I could tell you I have no fear of the outcome. . . . But owing to the concentration of our resources on fighting in Burma little has been done to strengthen the Chinese armies and for the same reason the 14th Air Force is still operating on a shoe string.

The Flying Tigers

The Japanese began their offensive the middle of April, 1944, and soon stabbed deeply into east China. Hengyang and other air bases were captured. In spite of this, Chennault kept hammering at Japanese shipping as he had promised. During the bitter battle for Kweilin his B-25s and fighters suddenly attacked a flotilla of merchant ships that had scurried to Hong Kong for refuge. Eight freighters were sunk and eleven damaged. Approximately 80,000 tons of shipping were destroyed in a single day.

Not long after this Kweilin fell. All China, apparently, was doomed. Stilwell was recalled to Washington.

The Japanese were now confident that Chennault had been thrown out of east China for good. But he was secretly building other airfields far from the enemy lines. Under the supervision of Henry Byroade, almost a million Chinese were constructing bomber and fighter strips. They broke rocks by hand and pulled five-ton rollers by sheer man power. In an incredibly short time, Chennault was again striking at the Japanese. He bombed Nanking, Hong Kong and then completely knocked out the great city of Hankow as a major base for the Japanese drive on central China.

The 14th Air Force was far from dead. December, 1944, was the greatest month in its history. Two hundred and forty-one planes were destroyed, and forty thousand tons of shipping were sunk. In addition, railroads were battered, thirty-seven locomotives being knocked out in a single day. The pilots also spotted 159 Japanese ships for United States submarines.

The spirit of the 14th Air Force, which had dropped understandably during the relentless Japanese advance into east China, had rebounded. Chennault's men now faced the enemy with the same confidence as the original Flying Tigers. Ed Rector was back and commanded the 23rd Fighter Group. Other AVG men had returned—Charles Older, Bill Reed, and George McMillan. Jack Chennault, the General's oldest son, was one of the fighter pilots.

At the beginning of 1945 Chennault increased his attacks. Canton and even Shanghai were blasted. Three hundred and thirty-four planes, a new record, were shot down in January. The number soon dropped but only because the enemy was becoming so weak. During April Chennault's fliers encountered only three enemy planes in the air. The Japanese had been knocked out of the China skies.

3.

In spite of this new succession of victories, Chennault's detractors in Washington were demanding that Lieutenant General G. E. Stratemeyer be placed in command of the Army Air Forces in China.

Chennault felt this cut his force to the size of a wing and that he would just be replacing one of his own wing commanders. Final victory was in sight; his job was done. He could do no more for the United States and China. He requested relief from active duty—and retirement from the Army.

He was proud of his 14th Air Force. In three years

General G. E. Stratemeyer pins the Distinguished Flying Cross on Major General Claire Chennault in recognition of his services as commander of the former Flying Tigers and as commander of the 14th U.S. Air Force in China.

it had lost only 468 planes while destroying almost 3,000. It had sunk and damaged 2,230,000 tons of enemy merchant shipping. Later Lieutenant General Takahashi, the Japanese commander in central China, would say, ". . . I judge the operations of the 14th Air Force to have constituted between sixty and seventy-five per cent of our effective opposition in China. Without the air force we could have gone anywhere we wished."

The man who had not possessed the "necessary qualifications for a successful aviator" and who was termed "prima donna" by his superiors had concluded one of the greatest careers in American military history. Despite repeated discouragements and the efforts of many important people to restrain him, he had never given up his dreams. Under the worst conditions, his unorthodox air combat tactics had set the highest air victory records in World War II.

He flew to Chungking to begin a farewell tour of his beloved China. The city was jammed with twice its normal population as he drove through the streets in Chiang Kai-shek's car. The crowds grew so great that the motor was switched off and the car was pushed by the people.

He got the same tumultous reception in Peishiyi, Sian, Chengtu, Luliang and Kunming. Every Chinese—rich and poor, merchant and laborer—wanted to see Old Leatherface. No other foreigner had so touched their hearts as "Chen-au-duh," the Flying Tiger.

But the men he left behind—the 14th Air Force—continued the battle against the Japanese, fighting as well as if he had still been their leader. These men, the last of the Flying Tigers, also won a place in the hearts of the Chinese. They would never be forgotten.

The fighting after Chennault's departure was brief. Less than two months after his resignation from the 14th Air Force, Japan surrendered. The Flying Tigers could well be proud of the part they had played in bringing about that surrender.

Bibliography

Ayling, Keith: *Old Leatherface of the Flying Tigers.* New York: Bobbs-Merrill Company, 1945.

Boyington, Gregory: *Baa Baa Black Sheep.* New York: G. P. Putnam's Sons, 1958.

Craven, W. F., and Cate, J. L. (Editors): *The Army Air Forces in World War II.* Volume 1. Plans and Early Operations, January 1939 to August 1942. Chicago: University of Chicago Press, 1948.

Greenlaw, Olga S.: *The Lady and the Tigers.* New York: E. P. Dutton and Company, Inc., 1943.

Gurney, Gene: *Five Down and Glory.* New York: G. P. Putnam's Sons, 1958. Paperback edition: Ballantine Books, Inc.

Hager, Alice Rogers: *Wings for the Dragon.* New York: Dodd, Mead and Company, 1945.

Haugland, Vern: *The AAF Against Japan.* New York: Harper and Row, Publishers, 1948.

Hotz, Robert B. (Editor): *Way of a Fighter; The Memoirs of Claire Lee Chennault.* New York: G. P. Putnam's Sons, 1949.

Hotz, Robert B., with the assistance of George L. Paxton and others: *With General Chennault; The Story of the Flying Tigers.* New York: Coward-McCann, Inc., 1943.

Loomis, Robert D.: *Great American Fighter Pilots of World War II.* A Landmark Book. New York: Random House, 1961.

Loomis, Robert D.: *The Story of the U.S. Air Force.* A Landmark Book. New York: Random House, 1959.

Romanus, Charles F., and Sunderland, Riley: *Stilwell's Command Problems.* Washington: Office of the Chief of Military History, Department of the Army, 1956.

Romanus, Charles F., and Sunderland, Riley: *Stilwell's Mission to China.* Washington: Office of the Chief of Military History, Department of the Army, 1953.

Scott, Robert L., Jr.: *Boring a Hole in the Sky.* New York: Random House, 1961.

Scott, Robert L., Jr.: *Damned to Glory.* New York: Charles Scribner's Sons, 1944.

Scott, Robert L., Jr.: *Flying Tiger: Chennault of China.* Garden City: Doubleday and Company, Inc., 1959.

Scott, Robert L., Jr.: *God Is My Co-pilot.* New York: Charles Scribner's Sons, 1944. Paperback edition: Ballantine Books, Inc.

Scott, Robert L., Jr.: *Tiger in the Sky.* New York: Ballantine Books, Inc., 1959.

Sims, Edward H.: *American Aces in Great Fighter Battles of World War II.* New York: Harper and Row, Publishers, 1958.

Toland, John: *But Not in Shame.* New York: Random House, 1961. Paperback edition: New American Library of World Literature, Inc.

Whelan, Russell: *The Flying Tigers.* New York: The Viking Press, 1943.

White, Theodore H. (Editor): *The Stilwell Papers.* New York: William Sloane Associates, 1948. Paperback edition: Macfadden-Bartell Corporation.

Bibliography

Unpublished Sources:

First American Volunteer Group Diary CBI, 1941–1942. The official AVG diary.

Gambay: The Story of the Fourteenth Air Force. An unpublished history compiled by a number of well-known authors for the Fourteenth Air Force.

History of Air Operations on the Continent of Asia, 1941–1946. Official U.S. Air Force History.

Also numerous after-action reports and other official documents.

Index

Index

Index

About the author of this book

JOHN TOLAND was born in La Crosse, Wisconsin, the son of a concert singer and an artist. He worked his way through Phillips Exeter Academy and Williams College—where he graduated Phi Beta Kappa in 1936—then studied playwriting at the Yale Drama School. During World War II he attended Officer Candidate School at Fargo, North Carolina, and later served in the Special Services Division of the Army. After the war, Mr. Toland came to New York and began a successful career as a free-lance writer. He has contributed to almost all the national magazines, including *American Heritage, Coronet, Reader's Digest* and *The Saturday Evening Post.*

Mr. Toland is the author of four adult books, two of which are about World War II: *But Not in Shame* and *Battle: The Story of the Bulge.* To obtain original material for these books—as he did for *The Flying Tigers* —Mr. Toland traveled extensively and interviewed a vast number of people.

U.S. LANDMARK BOOKS